AFTER

THE GRIEF JOURNEY AND WHAT TO EXPECT

Cheri A. Copie

Columbus, Ohio

The views and opinions expressed in this book are solely those of the author and do not reflect the views or opinions of Gatekeeper Press. Gatekeeper Press is not to be held responsible for and expressly disclaims responsibility of the content herein.

After: The Grief Journey And What To Expect

Published by Gatekeeper Press
2167 Stringtown Rd, Suite 109
Columbus, OH 43123-2989
www.GatekeeperPress.com

Copyright © 2021 by Cheri A. Copie
All rights reserved. Neither this book nor any parts within it may be sold or reproduced in any form or by any electronic or mechanical means, including information storage and retrieval systems, without permission in writing from the author. The only exception is by a reviewer, who may quote short excerpts in a review.

The editorial work for this book is entirely the product of the author. Gatekeeper Press did not participate in and is not responsible for any aspect of this element.

ISBN (paperback): 9781662909115
eISBN: 9781662909122

Dedication

First and foremost, this book is dedicated to my son Jordan's memory. He still lives on in my life, although we lost him suddenly. Our family had a choice: fall prey to the grasp of utter grief and bitterness or dust its pain off our shoulders and carry on. I am certain that Jordan would be immensely proud of this book because it is written expressly to care for others—just as he did when he was a paramedic. The lessons this young man of twenty-nine years showed me are countless and rich. Although we lost him, I am immensely grateful for the short time he was with us, as he made us all into a strong, resilient family. We are carrying on, Jordan!

I could not have imagined going through this life, with the loss of our son, without the steadfast love and support of my soulmate, Gary. After all the amazing years together, we never envisioned that life would throw us a curve ball as it did. Without your constant support, words of encouragement, and transparency, I would not be where I am today. You saved my life and are my rock. For that I will be forever grateful.

I could not have come through this nightmare without the amazing maturity and strength of my two sons, Justin and Taylor (TJ). You both carried me when I was at my weakest. This was not your job to parent me but as you always say, it is what it is. Your wisdom, resilience, and grace through our family's tragedy should be held up as an example for others to see. The pride I have for you both as the men you are today is indescribable. How you have taken my hand and walked this journey together with your dad and me while always finding Jordan-isms and joy is an amazing gift. I love you more than any mother is able. You are my greatest joy.

Finally, of the things I know for sure from living this life, I could not have triumphed over the immense pain and anguish of losing a child without the support of some special friends. You were the bedrock for our family. You innately knew what to do for not only me but the rest of my family. You stood out among all the others who tried to help us but found it awkward and difficult. You bravely went into the storm and pulled us out to safety when I'm sure it was difficult for you to do.

It is because of you that I wrote this book. You had the insight to know what to say, what not to say, what to do and what not to do for us – all at the amazingly perfect time. They say that true friends are those who stay with you when times are tough and you did. Our family will forever be in your debt. We are blessed to have you in our lives each and every day.

Grief is the price you pay for love.
—Queen Elizabeth II

Foreword

This book is meant to be a tool for all those who are silently suffering with loss or trying in a meaningful way to support someone with a loss. You are not alone in your feelings. You are surrounded by many who react and feel exactly as you do! What I have learned in my journey is to simply speak up. Share my thoughts aloud. Give a voice to the grief so that I can go through it successfully. Yes, you, too, can do this, but you need the support of folks around you. Let them in. Tell them your story. Speak of your loss and find eventual joy and meaning. *Yes, joy.*

There are breadcrumbs of gifts you will notice during your grief journey. There may even be signs that your loved one is still with you. Grieving is a deeply personal voyage laced with myriad emotions that simply need to be shared and felt. It's true that no two people experience grief in the same way. That's important to keep in mind as you experience it firsthand, because otherwise you may feel disappointed. There needs to be a foundation of understanding first.

You are feeling grief because you loved. That in itself is a wonderful gift. Feel grief's thorns. They are there because you had another human being in your life that touched your heart. That gift is to be celebrated, revered, and forever honored. Yes, it's true. Grief is the price you pay for loving. Embrace every moment. It is the tribute to the one lost. They earned it!

My hope for you, the reader, is that you find some snippets of identification and maybe an ah-ha moment here and there. During my grief journey, I didn't have anything real and poignant to reference then as I have created for you now or your loved one. I think that in the back of my mind, I've always wondered, "Is this feeling I have, normal?"

Read the book slowly and digest the messages that resonate. It is written solely from my personal grief journey. You will agree with some of the words and not with others. That's absolutely fine. Your journey will be different. Hopefully, there will be a time when you can share my words with someone else. It will highlight that they are not alone. We are in this together.

Table of Contents

Foreword — vii
Preface — x

The Backstory — 1
Jordan — 9
The Most Painful Moment — 17
Returning to the Unknown — 30
Dealing with Regrets — 38
Family Dynamics with Grieving — 43
Maneuvering to Survive — 53
When the World Seems to Go On Uninterrupted — 64
Dumb Things People Say — 68
Redefining Core Family Relationships — 78
Friendship Dynamics — 88
To Hell and Back—The Mid Stage — 91
Transitional Stage—Maturing and Self-Awareness — 96
Pet Loss — 104
The Firsts — 107
Social Media — 110
The New Normal: The Reinvention Stage — 113

About the Author — 120

*In an instant. Everything.
And then there is only the Before and After.*
–Anonymous

Preface

During the time I am writing this, our world is experiencing the coronavirus pandemic. Every nation must recognize the paralyzing effects that this crisis has bled into our lives. We will forever remember these days and be changed, just as much as some remember 9/11. There will be no going back to the way it once was because we have learned to adapt and survive into a newer normal. The days ahead are not certain, but it is thought that this nation will get back on its feet and be more invincible because of the way we are today.

Many reflections are posted on social media stating that we need to appreciate what we once had—especially the seemingly smaller things in life, such as toilet paper on the grocery shelves, attending large concerts, and the therapeutic value of receiving a warm hug. It is striking to me how much this resembles those who have experienced profound loss. This social crisis we have today feels oddly familiar, as if society is grieving *what was.*

While driving to the store early this a.m. to replenish our modest supplies, having been quarantined for week #2, I saw an ambulance pass by. It brought me to the realization that if my middle son, Jordan, were still alive, as a decorated paramedic he'd be on the front lines, doing whatever was needed. I know that I'd be terrified he'd get the virus and end up sick. But that was him—always to the rescue of others. Jordan was always first in line perhaps because of his unquenchable drive to fix things—a trait he inherited from his dad. This often put him in perilous situations, which brought me little comfort. Yet always laced with the mom anxiety was immense pride because my son was doing what he was passionate about. Many felt he was a hero. When the community was at its weakest, there Jordan would be standing. That was simply who he was. I know that today he'd be a leader in fighting this horrible pandemic.

I wrote this book to simply provide comfort, identification, and (if I'm lucky) hope to parents or loved ones who need to support those on a grief journey. I've walked in these shoes now for almost six years. When a woman loses her husband, she is called a widow. When a husband loses his wife, he is called a widower. When a child loses their parent, they are orphaned. However, when a parent loses a child or a sibling loses a brother or sister, there isn't a term. *Why is that?* Perhaps because it's unnatural to a degree, a *"let's don't go there"* situation and thus can't be understood easily.

Perhaps I'm naive, but I am a firm believer that people can't understand something *fully* until they have lived it. Grief is that way. Sure, we can say that we lost a grandparent or maybe even a parent. *But a child?* To lose a child, the feelings and collateral dynamics that result aren't immediately comprehensible—until you experience it or witness its grip.

I should preface my words here with the caveat that I am not a trained psychologist. I am not a mental health professional, and I do not possess degrees to bolster my expertise. I am a registered nurse, which only provides me practical, almost mechanical, expertise—all with the goal of healing, restoring, and preserving life. Death was not an option for the patients I had. Yet maybe because of my clinical background, I should have seen the signs clearer when there was trouble ahead.

What I can tell you is that I am, firsthand, a victim of the grip of grief. A warrior on the front lines. I've felt my heart and my head being ripped to shreds by an invisible tyrant called grief. Admittedly, I wrestle with this monster every day. What I have been able to do is get stronger and more resolute with life's events. I've

Preface

learned immense lessons and have stumbled terribly along the way with my attempts to return to normal.

This goal is to assist the reader in recognizing the myriad feelings that arise and embracing them instead of burying or dismissing them. This book may also help guide those folks who are not necessarily on the grief road, but maybe the sidewalks as support onlookers. I am a mom who has traversed the most painful event possible, with good moments, dark moments, and many in-between. I have learned abundant, valuable lessons throughout this journey and wanted to share them. Some words may resonate, and others won't. That is entirely fine.

Everyone's grief journey is different. There's no right or wrong journey. It simply is. I felt that there were limited resources when I needed them. My husband and I had nothing. That simply can't be. Some information shared is lessons learned. Some might be candid emotions. But primarily these words are to be points of reality and light for anyone struggling with loss. The important thing is that I have emerged a stronger individual because of my pain. I'm someone I didn't know I ever could be. I cling to these milestones because today I feel resilient, authentic, and balanced. It takes time, though.

Like the coronavirus pandemic, loss will bring us to our knees, strip us of all ego and strength, yet allow us to rebuild in a stronger way if we choose to do so. This is my personal story to share, with hopes of telling you, the reader, that you can get through the awful days. You simply need to consciously force yourself to look for the collateral beauty and gifts along the way, every day. It is a choice. Not a natural one by any means, because I'd rather crawl into bed with the covers over my head and hug my pup. But I realize that's not healthy.

Let your unhappiness and frustrations be your fuel to break your vicious cycles.
–Trina Hall

The Backstory

We have a motto in our family, which is: "Understand the backstory behind important issues." To know the backstory lends perspective and insight. Otherwise, we just have a lens to the surface. To that end, it's important that you understand the backstory of our family's life.

I was brought up in a traditional family in Upstate New York. My parents had the best of intentions in raising their three daughters, but I have come to believe that some adults should not be parents. I'd say my mother was one of these folks. She was a woman before her time and obsessed with all sorts of business adventures during a time when women were expected to be full-time mothers and homemakers. She craved attention constantly and perhaps had narcissistic tendencies (but again, I am not a clinical therapist). Mom and Dad stayed together because of us kids, but their marriage suffered because of it.

I am a firm believer of two things: parents do the best job they can, and children often do not know anything different. While I certainly did not have any healthy role models on what being a good mother was, I was convinced that if given that opportunity, I would stop the dysfunctional cycle in which I was stuck. My father was a very successful man in business yet remained passive and tolerant at home just to keep a semblance of peace as much as he could. I chose to feel no resentment toward them. I felt it in my bones that there had to be more, such as being a parent who had children who felt safe and loved at all times. I personally don't feel it is my job as a mom to judge who they are as individuals. As long as they are good people in society, and happy, that was my goal.

The Backstory

I was fortunate enough to meet my husband, Gary, in the late seventies. He was, and still is, my direct opposite. I am proud to say that, after forty-two years, he is my soul mate, and I would choose him again in a heartbeat. I am grateful every day to wake up next to him, share our life together, and fall asleep together in the evening. To this day, I have no clue why our marriage works as well as it does, but I am immensely grateful for being able to share my life with him and raise our three sons together as a team. He's a man of integrity.

When I became a mom to boys, I was in a foreign land. Not only was I totally ignorant of the male psyche, *I didn't want boys!* I'd envisioned being a mom to girls. When my second son was born, they called a social worker into the labor room because I was crying, having learned that I had given birth to another boy. I was immensely disappointed when Jordan was born. When we learned about my surprise pregnancy ten years later, my husband said that maybe this was going to be our little girl finally. Nope. Not happening. Taylor John (TJ) was born to complete our family in 1993.

As a mother, I wanted to be always present, fun, and available to my children as much as humanly possible. Looking back, this desire was most likely the result of trying to fill the void from my own childhood. I adored these four men in our household, who had decidedly different personas, temperaments, and interests. It is true when they say each child is different. What you don't hear is that each child gives the parent different gifts because of who they are with you! I worked through their childhoods but did so in a way that they were always my priority. My schedules would work around them. I didn't miss their functions or games, and we somehow all made it work wonderfully!

My oldest, Justin, is a driven and a methodical risk taker. He tirelessly played with Legos, creating structures from his head that should have been marketed by the Lego kit department. He is immensely creative. He was the child we "experimented" on because we didn't have role models to rely upon. We brought him up as authentically as possible, with reasonable goals. He didn't need to bring home A's. He simply needed to do always do his best. Today, he is a great son by all measures. He eventually bought his own IT company and is running it in contrarian ways. To watch Justin lead his organization today is truly the best show on this planet.

My second son, Jordan, was the dreamer—introverted and surreally empathetic since grade school. His sensitivity and kindness were second to no one else I knew. He enjoyed being alone growing up and spent time outdoors more than indoors. He said that fishing gave him time to be with himself, and that was

The Backstory

why he loved it so much. He was an amazing baseball player, golfer, and briefly wanted to be a chef. That all fell by the wayside when he volunteered at the local ambulance district. He became a credentialed EMT and quickly rose through the ranks at an ambulance company as their battalion chief at the young age of twenty-seven. We all knew that after a "bad call" that he'd been on, we needed to give him his space for a day or so he could process and re-center. Jordan was beautifully complicated and fragile in many ways. But his grace and sensitivity made our family appreciate the fragility of life itself.

Our youngest son, TJ, was our surprise after many years of trying. He is incredibly tenacious, wise beyond his years, and has an itch to explore all that life has to offer. If I had to pick one word, it would be *fearless*. It didn't surprise us when he decided to travel to Costa Rica alone at age twenty-four just to see the country. TJ doesn't fully honor life's boundaries all the time. There's always more he wants to experience and see. There are no limits. Yet TJ keeps much of what he feels tucked inside and rarely allows others to see the real him. Yet when his guard is down, it pours out like a gift. His circle is tight, but those closest to him are allowed to see a beautiful soul spill out, excited with life's potential.

As the boys got older, our life developed into a cadence of rituals, such as Sunday dinners, cigars on the back deck, and a familial language including nicknames. Humor infiltrated every encounter, and we all knew that we should never feel uncomfortable in our own home—even for an instant. When they moved out, they knew that the refuge our home offered them would always be there. Many times, I'd be lying on my bed upstairs, minding my own business, when one of them (now grown) would come tramping through on my clean white carpet with their work shoes on, plop on the bed, and say, *"What cha watching, Ma?"* We'd end up talking for quite a while, just on everyday things, and then they'd leave to their respective homes. I look back on those moments and realize that these were everyday gifts.

During these years, my faith was moderately strong; yet I was not necessarily as staunch a Catholic as I had been raised. I had a belief in God, absorbed the concept of karma, and felt that if you gave to others in an unselfish way and tried to be a solidly good human being, life would reward you with good things. I earnestly believed good reaped good. Just prior to Jordan passing, I had come into a life habit of doing one kind thing a day for someone else. Think about it: I had to think beyond myself, see someone else's need, and unselfishly help them. There were big things I'd do, and then there might be smaller things on other days. Every day, a kindness was shown. I wasn't a saint but felt that I had become a solidly good and kind person.

I was immensely grateful for my life and never took a second for granted. I was appreciative of my husband being there for me in every possible way while treasuring these three lives that we were responsible for raising the best way we knew how. I adore my boys! Most importantly, I was able to become a mother that I would have envied myself in nearly every capacity. No regrets. To this day, if asked what my greatest accomplishment was, I would answer that I was a good mom. I was fun, safe to confide in, reliable, creative, and limitless in my love for each one of them. My life had a peaceful cadence.

In 2014, all that changed.

> *We are all human but in no way are we the same. We all have things that make us individual and unique. There is a story behind every one of us, a reason why we are the way we are.*
> –Anonymous

Jordan

I might sound shallow, but I thought I'd be a better mom to girls. I knew how girls thought, what they wanted, and understood the myriad emotions a female goes through. I envisioned being close to a daughter someday. I'd coach her through the dating years, help her with her wedding, be there when she had children of her own, and would guide her through marriage, parenthood, and life in general. Having a daughter would put me in a place of familiarity and identity.

When we had our first son, Justin, I was grateful. It would be new to me and provided my husband, Gary, with the masculine perpetuity for the family name. Gary was thrilled and I was overcome with absolute joy at being a mom. Two years later came Jordan. I was not as thrilled, admittedly, because we had planned on having just two children, and my prospects of having a little girl were now extinguished like a winded flame.

Sometimes when life throws you a curveball, it's a blessing in disguise.

Jordan ended up being *my* son. I say that with all candor because there are children that intuitively understand one parent over another, without words. There's a tighter connection with that one parent, which simply can't be described. Sometimes, it's a transient phenomenon, and for other families it's an unspoken code. Jordan was mine. In later years, he would call me on the phone while I was at work, astutely listen to how I'd say "hello," and say, "Ma, what's wrong?" He'd always had that intuitive gift of sensing how folks were feeling. He loved medicine as I did and loved animals to a fanatical degree, admittedly as I am today. We just "got" each other without much effort.

He was not an easy child, by any means. He was markedly different from Justin, who embraced life enthusiastically and was audacious. Jordan was more comfortable in the background and an introvert. He was highly sensitive and lived in his mind more so than others. I would say that Jordan was always comfortable in his own skin. He didn't feel that he needed to prove anything to anyone. He was his own fan base.

However, because he walked to the tune of a different drummer, he would often be bullied and ostracized. His grade school and high school years were very difficult because he wanted to fit in somehow but didn't have the grace or ability to "play the game" to blend in with others well. It was awkward for him to follow the crowd, which later would be the same quality that helped him rise in the ranks of his career.

Jordan was a big kid. He grew to six foot three inches and had a very large physical presence when he walked into the room. The first thing you'd notice was his crystal blue eyes, perfectly angled nose, and a smooth baby face. It would not be an exaggeration to say that he would be considered quite good-looking and a force to be reckoned with if he was confronted. He suffered from allergies, which made his lips pillow out. It only added to his softness when looking at such a large physique. We called him Tuckey, Jordie, Chunk, and other fond names that highlighted his personality. He had my family's appetite and metabolism genes because he was the brother that was predisposed to

gain weight. However, he would be able to slim down just as easily (which was a gift I envied).

In high school he found his passion and societal family. He volunteered at Penfield Volunteer Ambulance, became an EMT, and then continued to become a battalion chief at age twenty-seven for an ambulance company in Rochester, New York. His gift of empathy and intuitive insight made him a decorated medic with an array of specialized certifications. We were immensely proud! Little did we know that this successful direction in life would become his demise.

Jordan battled depression on and off but was responsible enough to seek professional care and treatment. He would go on calls, some of which were the most gruesome and horrid to see. Proficiently, he'd tend to the victims, come home, and we'd know he'd be quiet for at least the next forty-eight hours while he processed all that he saw. Day after day, he'd go in, lead his teams bravely, and care for the most fragile. If I were to guess, I'd say one out of every fifty calls would "hit him." One in particular was a small baby pulled from a swimming pool, whom he'd frantically tried to rescue. He had his own son at that time, Kaiden, and that experience never left him. In retrospect, that was probably the beginning of the end.

Shortly around that time, he had an accident in which equipment fell onto his back, requiring long-term pain management. Several years passed, and we thought nothing of it since he rarely showed any evidence that it was lingering. He had a high pain tolerance and rarely complained about anything. He was prescribed OxyContin and other pain meds, including fentanyl patches. Without a clue to us, he'd become addicted. When the prescriptions were discontinued, he went to the street. Piecing together his history of addiction later, we learned that Jordan most likely thought he could beat his addiction on his own.

He met Kate, a nurse, who was his soul mate. Kate had a way with Jordan, accepting him for exactly who he was. She really didn't care to change him in any great way and enjoyed the excitement he'd bring to their relationship with his passion for saving others and his relentless off-color humor. Jordan was an acquired taste. Kate was his partner who was willing to face with him anything life had ahead.

They were married and had a beautiful boy named Kaiden (a mix of Kate and Jordan). Life was good. Then slowly Jordan's personality became a bit jaded and unpredictable. We all attributed it to the nature of his work and tried to adapt and not rock his boat. In retrospect, life was giving us a red flag. What we all learned is that if a person's personality changes quickly and dramatically, that should not be rationalized away. You might want to make up excuses, but you are deceiving yourself. We all saw his temperament change and decided to dance around it. We dismissed our gut

reactions when they needed to be heard the most! Sadly, as a family, we were in unison on what we saw.

The erratic moods got to be too much, so Kate needed time away. They agreed to live apart while trying to work on their marriage, for Kaiden's sake. We all agreed that this was a prudent plan. Yet none of us knew that there was another entity in their marriage, and that was addiction. Kate had no chance until the insidious homewrecker left the relationship. To think of addiction as another being in the relationship fits best. It was the "mistress" in their marriage. It was expensive, kept secret, and yet so enjoyable to Jordan that he couldn't quit.

I, too, saw the personality change. Jordan had never been upset with me through all his years. He was my kindest son. Yet nearly twelve months prior to his death, he became angry at dinner, standing up to spar with Gary on a trivial issue with an exaggerated fury. It was shocking. I then stood up between them to break it up. Jordan looked into my eyes from six inches away with utter rage. What I also noticed at that very second was that his eyes were vacant. Life was giving us yet another red flag. I knew at that moment, for whatever reason, I was losing my son. To what, or why, I did not know. As his mom, I also didn't have any control.

The last several months of Jordan's life was like that out of a B-rated movie. As parents, Gary and I learned the "tough love" strategy where you need to hold firm and set limits with consequences to follow. It is a sound parenting strategy but may be counterintuitive with a person under the influence.

The erratic behavior, mood swings, emotional distance, and anger spread in all aspects of his life, culminating in him being dismissed from his job at the ambulance company. That devastated him. Because he didn't finish college, he sought other careers and landed on studying to become an insurance salesperson. Yet the seduction of drug use, separation from Kate, and isolation turned him into a heroin addict. *Well hidden.*

Jordan would ask us for money, which we turned over since he wasn't employed, only to later learn we were funding his addiction. His brother had to call the police to have him committed because of the behaviors. He was an inpatient for a few days and discharged with the prescription of treatment by a therapist. I took responsibility for him when discharged, and once I got him home, he dismissed me. He assured me that he'd contact Kate and together we'd all get through this. It didn't feel right then, and I chose to ignore it. Third red flag.

Kate and Jordan seemed to be reconciling. I chose to believe it was a fresh start ahead. It was to be a Christmas to remember.

There is no pain so great as the memory of joy in present grief.
—Aeschylus

The Most Painful Moment

By all accounts, Christmas 2014 was going to be special. Two of our three sons were coming down from New York State to us in Florida to visit us for the holiday. Jordan decided to remain in New York to be with his son, then two, and wife. He was getting his life back together. Justin was coming in on an early Christmas Day flight, and TJ was to come down later in the afternoon.

I texted Jordan on Christmas Eve to simply check in and wish him and his family well. At 6:30 pm Jordan replied that he wished the same for us. Gary and I went to dinner that evening, anticipating our other sons' visit the next day. Little did we know that that was to be the last meal within the normal life that we all knew to appreciate.

At 8:30 am on Christmas Day my phone rang. I answered it, thinking it was Jordan asking me to watch our grandson open his presents on FaceTime. However, on the other end was his best friend asking if I could put the phone on speaker for Gary to hear. Together we heard the words that will absolutely devastate any parent. *"I'm sorry. I'm here at Jordan's place and he has passed."*

His wife had found him in his easy chair, cold, with residue around his mouth and obviously deceased. Next to him lay a spoon, matches, a baggie, and a tourniquet. Our son had died from an accidental overdose. This was nothing less than a nightmare. *When am I going to wake up from this awful dream?*

Hearing the words that my baby boy was gone wreaked physical havoc on every metabolic function I had at that moment. I fell to my knees, cried a guttural sound, screaming what was the only thought I had: "WHY?" Within a few minutes, I was vomiting into the toilet. Some say that the experience of finding out your child has passed is the worst thing a parent can experience. At that moment, I understood. I felt my mind whirling around and wanting to pull me back from his horrible nightmare. *This can't be! This must be a mistake.* Yet it wasn't.

All in an instant, my life catapulted into a place of destroyed understanding on so many things. The loss of a child that I carried, understood and cherished does feel like your heart is being ripped out of your chest. But to lace that with the circumstances of him dying at the hands of street drugs was insurmountable to accept. My sheltered life of heroin and oxycontin was that only homeless folks under downtown bridges would die of that – certainly not a decorated paramedic who knew better! He watched junkies die in his arms on a routine basis. None of this made sense. Later down the road, Gary and I became educated about the grip street drugs has on every type of person around us. It's a silent, unspoken pandemic of sorts that needs to be addressed. For now, we needed to simply find a morsel of strength to function. At that particular moment in time on that Christmas morning, our focus was to get to our boys, Kate and Kaiden.

We were unable to intercept our oldest son, who was flying at that moment, but we were able to book three tickets to return to Rochester and told our third son to stay put. The logistics of getting to Jordan in New York under this shroud of disbelief and utter pain was like running in drying cement. There are little things I remember of that morning, like showering with tears running down my face, digging through my strongbox for any of his records I might have, and the smell of the taxi that took us to the airport. We met Justin at the arrival gate in the airport, gave him the news, and turned him right back around onto a return flight. The three of us were ashen and stoic. I remember being in the bulkhead seats aimlessly staring ahead at the torn pockets with curled magazines on the wall. We flew without words. None of this made sense.

20

We arrived in Rochester by dinnertime Christmas Day and met up with TJ. My husband got on the phone with the local police to see if there were any pieces we could assemble, which could have made us miraculously feel better. The story was grim. With impassive citations from the police captain on the phone, we learned our son definitely passed sometime the night before, likely caused by an overdose of heroin. *Heroin? Isn't that what homeless folks use under a downtown bridge?* Everything that I believed was imploding. At the time, I categorized that conversation as being the most painful moment of my life.

Thankfully we had friends in the funeral business who swooped in to care for our son. He was at the medical examiner's office, and we were told that "soon they would be done." *Done with what?* They were required to perform an autopsy to identify the cause of death. Being a nurse, I knew that every inch of his body was being opened for any possible clue. I called our friends and pleaded to get him back as soon as possible. The thought of him being on a stainless table with bright lights, drains, recorders, hoses, and scales surrounding him, only to then be tucked into a refrigerated compartment, seemed utterly cruel to my mind. *This was my baby boy. How could this be happening! This for sure will now rank as the most painful moment of my life.*

The Most Painful Moment

The following days were the worst in my life. My husband was amazingly strong, as was my oldest son. I was now without strength, function, reason, or energy. Depleted would be a good word, although sadly an understatement. We went to the funeral home to pick out his casket, decided whether he was to be buried or cremated, arranged for the services, and selected meaningless holy cards to hand out. All of it seemed immensely trivial. Yet necessary. The calls had to be made—all with the scripted responses of: *"I am so sorry." "How did this happen?"* and *"Let me know what I can do to help."* Then the scramble to make poster boards of this wonderful man's life. *Really? Poster boards summarizing an amazing man's accomplishments? I don't know where all the pictures are—why are you asking me to do this now?* However, the "doing" of these things provided purpose to those around me. The mission was to give Jordan a service that would celebrate the beautiful life he'd had. So, I went through the motions. I remember being in the basement pulling his baby book and albums to use, wiping tears from my already swollen eyes, just to pick the right photos. This was the hardest part of losing a child. *Surely,* I thought, *this is the most painful moment of my life.*

There were immediate practical decisions to be made. Was he to be buried or cremated? Where should we bury him? What steps did we need to take to make the myriad arrangements? There was also a curiosity—a need—to find out whom he'd last communicated with, what his last moments were like, and a desire to put the pieces of Humpty Dumpty back together again. Perhaps having insight as to what his last minutes were like would bring us closure. We learned that cellular companies are unable to help under these circumstances. We needed to try password after password for his cell phone until we were successful. I choose to believe that it was Jordan's magic that led my son to the right password. *The not knowing,* I thought, *certainly was the most painful moment of my life.*

The day of the wake with its calling hours came with dread. We arrived early to find Jordan lying regally in his magnificent casket in the suit my husband carefully picked out and delivered. I walked into the room packed with overly pungent floral arrangements and soft lighting. As I walked up to him, I got fifteen feet away and both of my legs buckled. My friend, the funeral director, knew this would happen apparently, because she was right there, holding me up. Yet I fell to the ground like a slaughtered animal. They needed to pull me up from the floor. *This is real.* Jordan was there in front of me, but gone. I think it was then that I surrendered to the reality this was not a nightmare. *This had to be the most painful moment of my life.*

The Most Painful Moment

When I walked up to him, I saw serous fluid draining from the concealed autopsy incision on the back of his head and tried to cover it as any good mother would do. He didn't look at all like he did alive. His lips were thin and bland, his skin was white with pallor, and his exquisite crystal-blue eyes not at all open. The reality of who is was at that moment was indeed the worst part of losing a child. *This is now the most painful moment of my life.*

Little did we know that the wake was a gift! I tell that to everyone who walks in these shoes today. *Yes, it's true, a gift.* At the wake, we learned all the facets of our son that he'd never shared with us. The stories, the memories, tributes of gratitude, and true appreciation from total strangers were there to help us through these days. I remember getting into the car with my husband afterward and saying, *"Who was our son? I'm so amazed at who he was at his core! The things he never shared but did for those in need. Why didn't he tell us?"* While I'm sure I don't remember much of what folks shared, it was one of those times where society tried to carry us with love. For that, I will forever be grateful.

One of the biggest surprises was learning that Jordan had dressed up as Batman for a frail elderly patient he brought to the hospital. Apparently, the woman was alone and scared, and the only way to calm her was to talk about the superhero constantly till they reached the emergency department. A few days later, the story goes, Jordan squeezed his hefty body into the spandex costume and found that woman. The joy he brought her was palpable to the entire nursing staff! Jordan never told us he'd done this.

There was an observation during that evening that we recount to others as well. Many will come through the endless line and say, *"If there's anything you need, please call."* We were all trained that this was the right thing to say, and certainly appreciated the gesture, but we knew we'd never reach out or ask for anything. We also learned later that nearly all the folks in the wake's line craved information as to what had happened. Justin overheard many speculating as they stood in line. While we understood the natural tendency and curiously, there was a part of us that felt violated.

Then there were several folks who would come through, saying, *"We will be dropping off a dish or homemade meal, and if you don't need, you can toss it."* They didn't need to do anything but knew it would help in some small way. They respected our pain and could identify what we needed. Perhaps it was because they walked similar paths or just knew what helped and what didn't. It was those folks who had the intuitive ability to soothe. This was a great lesson for us in that we now know what to do going forward when we comfort those who have lost.

Finally, there were a very select group of close friends who came through the line with no words. Their tears covered their red, puffy eyes. With no words, they gave us hugs that never quit. *Those* were the ones who truly understood our pain. You see, they, too, had lost Jordan in their lives. While they said nothing, they told us volumes. For those select few, we were immensely comforted. They fed our souls at that moment. Later we would realize that those were our truest of friends to help us on this journey for the many years ahead—this was truly a gift.

We learned a valuable lesson at that same time. Folks will ask what happened more out of curiosity than anything. *I get it!* A twenty-nine-year-old son doesn't just pass away. There had to be more to it, and they simply wanted to know. Looking back, the reality was that our experience of loss was projecting onto others as being *their* worst fear. Maybe the logic is that if they could understand what happened with our son, then they would be able to further protect their family so it wouldn't happen to them.

With the ubiquity of social media, the speculation was rampant. Because you don't know who is linked with whom, messages will surface unintentionally to the most fragile of viewers. What folks need to realize is that when this happens to those who grieve, the family feels an emotional violation. Although unintentional and without malice, the gaping wound is opened wider. This was the most painful moment of losing our child because our privacy was now extinguished.

The lesson we learned to rehearse is to politely say his heart simply stopped. Later, we would add to that valuable lesson: we'd only share Jordan's story with those who had earned the right to know. At the time, we were grappling with what might have happened, so it would be impossible for us to share with anyone else what had occurred. All it provided us were feelings of exposure and vulnerability at a time where we had no protective shield. I understand human curiosity and concern. Yet when it's an untimely death, the questions can feel like bullets to the cracked veneer of privacy. To us, the question always came down to *"Why is it that he/she wants to know?"* Death is not about the community as much as it's about comforting the immediate family. If the people around the grieving could keep that in their minds at all times, it would steer appropriate actions. This was a great lesson!

It was years later that our daughter in law Kate pointed out that those early days during the wake and burial, she felt immensely embarrassed for her less than ideal behavior. I had no idea what she was referring to as we always saw her to be a woman of profound grace and resilience. She said that on many occasions during the burial days, she snapped back at people. Her filters were off. I promptly reminded her that she was doing everything in her ability to remain afloat during these rough seas. Yet, she did say that it was a great lesson learned because now she knows to anticipate that on occasion from others who would succumb to the grips of utter grief.

We buried our son with numb motions laced with regal words on a blistery, cold, grey day. We all felt sick to our stomachs and wanted this to just be over. The tears teetered at the edge of our eyes and yet we needed to handle ourselves with appropriate social decorum just to get through the task at hand, which was to bury Jordan. We needed to follow a regimen, listen to endless but kind words by others, and maneuver what our new family dynamic would be after all others had left.

A few weeks later, when we had the strength, we decided it was time to discard his personal things. The situation at the time of his death was that Jordan was separated from his wife, Kate. She'd moved out and found a place of her own prior to December. That left his townhouse with all his personal possessions. Walking into his place had an eerie feel. It was as if Jordan was still there, because we could smell him. At that moment, I loved that scent and wished it to never leave my memory. But we needed to get to work and go through his clothes, fishing gear, tools, kitchen items, and precious golf clubs. I don't know where our family got the strength to do all this, but we were able to empty his place enough to sell it. I remember the last few minutes at his home, looking back into the empty rooms and feeling as if Jordan had evaporated. His scent was no longer to be found. It was a chapter closed. *This became the most painful moment of my life.*

The reality was that a huge piece of us was now gone. Jordan remained in our hearts, but he wasn't there for us to see, touch, smell, or engage. His relentless sick humor was now silenced. His ability to incessantly recite movie lines with his brother was now void of the partner.

I realized quickly after Jordan's funeral that my boys' mother was no longer able to be there for them. I was vacant with emotions and struggled to maintain balance for myself, let alone for my husband or sons. It felt akin to being in the ocean with only my lifejacket on, treading water while watching the rest of my family bob up and down in their jackets just to stay afloat. It was torture to see those men that I love so deeply grieve alone without their wife or mom to help them. Yet I was paralyzed. The chains of grief had such a grip on me that I was frozen. Just to get through a simple day was arduous. I could only watch them struggle alone. *This was now the most painful moment of losing a child.*

The Most Painful Moment

How many times can you watch your son die? Six months passed and I received something in my email. It was from a local government address, so I opened it. It was Jordan's autopsy results. Reading it alone, unprepared, with my burning tearing eyes, it was clear that they dissected every organ, weighed its parts, and depicted the status of each item examined with officious clinical verbiage. Reading the report, I was able to follow their procedure, step by step. I was there in the sterile room as the medical examiner dictated the information. I could see it all. My son died of an accidental overdose. That now was the most painful moment. I wanted to vomit. *This was the most painful moment of my life.*

*Question Everything. Learn Something.
Answer Nothing.*
–Euripides

Returning to the Unknown

You might think that after raising three boys, moving to Florida, and living a predictable older adult life, the opportunity to question *"what's next?"* would wane. Our life was settled in a tidy bucket of routine and order. However, when you grieve, you are placed in a world of reckless uncertainty, labile emotions, and deliberate isolation. You feel your heart broken into millions of pieces, and life as you knew it is shattered. All that you once thought to be true prior to your loss is now scattered. If I were to draw a picture of how it feels, I would be sketching a small, unsteady boat in the middle of endless ocean, trying to stay afloat. You have no compass or landmarks. It's a matter of just surviving.

I remember my husband and me saying to each other, *"Maybe we need to give this just a little bit more time and things will return to normal. We can do this! If we return to work, reengage with our friends, perform our rituals and routines, and do familiar things prior to losing Jordan, it will all come back to us."* That would be the way we'd heal. Looking back, it was the epitome of our naiveté. We had no benchmarks.

I did seek counseling by two different providers because I knew I couldn't dig out of this myself. My husband couldn't help me, so we needed to rely on those skilled to pull us out. But what I learned quickly was that unless they, too, experienced grief as I was feeling, it was not going to be productive. I remember one counselor listening to me blubber away about my pain only to have her suggest that maybe journaling would help. While I applaud the work of clinical psychotherapists, the work around the massive grips of grieving, for some, can only be provided by kindred victims. Unfortunately, I did not find a therapist at that time who gave me the impetus to move forward in a positive direction. What I did find was the typical recommendations for journaling, being physically active, and trying to communicate my feelings to whomever I would be in contact with. These are all prudent interventions to consider, but I was looking for the magic bullet to fix how I felt and pull me back from the precipice of myself falling into an abyss from which I'd never return. I have never felt more out of control than at that moment in time.

When I speak to other parents surviving loss, they all ask the same question within the first ten minutes of our initial conversation. They ask, *"When will we return to normal?"* We have heard countless others consoling, gently patting their shoulders while saying, *"Just give it time. You will get there."* Gary and I don't say this. In our opinion, to say that to a grieving person is providing them potential for false hope. If a grieving person has the courage to ask you the question, they deserve the right to know the honest answer. You see, they cling to your answer, and if normal doesn't return to them (which it won't), the grieving person feels like they have failed.

The truth to loss is that what you had before is no longer. What one knew to be real once is now gone. They need to realize that so that they aren't searching to regain it down the road. I gently tell these broken souls that what they had is in the past. Instead, I offer them the concept to reinvent their present while respecting the loss. Accept the reality as it is and build from there a new normal. While the listener does not want to hear this, they all seem to believe it readily. After a few years of helping other families, I do feel that they know it already in their gut, but no one could give a voice to this.

The other statement that always surfaces is what I call the "woulda-coulda-shouldas." The "if onlys." *"If I had called them, this wouldn't have happened." "If I knew he was in pain, I could have helped him."* Essentially, they're saying if circumstances were somehow altered in a trivial way, the fate of what happened would never have occurred. Other comments center on that there's a chance it could have been prevented, and, in some way, they are at some level responsible. When I hear these things, I listen with respect because it's a way for them to process.

But then I gently state that it is unfair for them to think that they had such a profound impact on fate. Perhaps the death could have been avoided, but the series of events that were real, to risk the fatal result, did not allow it to happen. I've always brought my boys up to believe that blame was a useless action. It changes nothing. So, you assign blame—then what? Did the outcome change? Did it make one feel better? Not really. Blame is a placeholder for productive time toward healing. The woulda-coulda-shouldas are a prime example of wasted energy. If not now, it might have happened later under worse circumstances. It was not something you could have controlled.

Other questions surface, which will be touched on later in this book. At some level, I questioned all that I ever believed when loss arrived. Karma. Fairness. Doing the right thing. Grace. Faith (a big one). Relationships. Life in general. Everything was challenged. Some aspects may get stronger. Others may change totally. We as humans try to integrate logic and balance in our lives. But with death, it's nearly impossible. Yet to process the situation, I suspect that it's natural to question aspect and is part of the process. Embrace it. Remember when I wrote that the initial shock of the news made your mind whirl? I've come to believe that the processing of the relentless questions weeks or months later is our way to cycle back our minds into what we can carry on with for that time. My hope is that the new grief awareness programs have this integrated on every level.

Being more pragmatic, let's consider the questions by society. Everyone will be asking *"What happened?"* While they come from a place of benign curiosity more than anything else, it feels like invasion of privacy to the one grieving. The one who has lost someone feels incredibly vulnerable. Why add to this? In my case, I didn't know what had happened for many weeks! If I didn't know, how on Earth could I share this information? Then growth came almost immediately when we discovered that they ask just to fill their curiosity bucket. I remember trying to tell countless folks about Jordan, only to be met with flat, one-word replies and a prompt change of subject. Maybe I'd made the listener uncomfortable. Maybe I'd said something too real. Maybe that's not what they expected to hear. Whatever it was made me feel emotionally exposed and now empty and frankly foolish. There was nothing to be gained if I told you. Absolutely no productive payoff for me the wounded. It was a useless, invasive activity to my deepest privacy. Our family quickly learned that we would tell no one Jordan's story unless they earned the right to know. In the meantime, the answer would be "his heart stopped." In this period of our lives, I mention this concept repeatedly that we learned the lesson of self-protection and safety.

The one question I heard often was *"How are you?"* I knew that folks didn't really want to know of the tangled dark emotions under the surface of my skin. I was exhausted from trying to be stronger than I truly felt. If I told them (which I did only a few times), they wouldn't know how to reply. So, I would politely answer that I was doing as well as could be expected under the circumstances, hoping every day would be better. They felt satisfied that they were doing the right thing asking and I felt protected by not really sharing.

Yet the gift I received during the immediate loss of Jordan came from my young assistant at the office, Steve. There he was every day before I arrived. He was the same age as Jordan. Every morning, he'd have my office prepared, my lights on, and always so welcoming. I'd come into the office, sit at my desk, and within ten minutes this wise-beyond-his-years young man would come in and ask, *"How are you, really?"* It's amazing what the added six-letter word adds to the question, but it came from a place of authenticity, caring, and concern. I knew I could tell Steve anything that I was feeling. On the bad days, he'd close my door and protect it like a gargoyle outside. I will forever be grateful for this gift. I later learned that he had experienced deep grief and could relate to an empathetic degree. He was my gift.

One seemingly easy question to answer prior to Jordan's death was *"How many kids to you have?"* After Jordan passed away, that has remained to be a difficult question to provide a reply. Only once did I reply *"Two."* Instantly, I felt the rush of guilt and betrayal against Jordan and knew at my core that this was not to be the answer I would ever use again. I have three sons. Jordan still is my boy and I will not eliminate that fact from my being and existence. What I have learned to say now is something like: *"I have a son who is 38, one who would be 36 and another who is 26."* The observation is that 99.9% of the time, listeners aren't really astute to pick up on the inference that one is no longer. They move on with their subsequent light conversation.

Finally, the one question the grieving ask themselves without any resolution most often is *"Why me?"* I asked that a million times and never had the answer that would put it to bed. There is no answer. A few years down the road, I heard someone bring it up and reply, *"Why not you?"* I said that it wasn't fair! I was a good person! I didn't deserve such heartache. But what I was indirectly saying is that I thought others *did deserve* such a battle.

Perhaps I was given this pain to change the direction of my life where it would help others. Perhaps

I was given this challenge because in some twisted way, I could handle it. Perhaps this is no rhyme or reason with fate, and I was just next in line. I still don't have the right answer for "why me?" and I expect I never will. I remember being obsessive and relentless to get an adequate answer. Yet it never came. What I did realize is that I can't dwell on it. It will make me bitter. I also soon came to realize that everyone carries around their demons and hurts. This one, for us, just was more visible to the world. I need to choose things during this journey—choose to believe signs, choose to believe meanings, and choose how I will react and behave. I wasn't always like this, but now it is one of my strongest attributes, which I carry every day. An overused saying comes to mind, which fits perfectly—*"It is what it is."*

*No regrets doesn't mean living with courage.
It means living without reflection. To live without
regret is to believe you have nothing to learn.
You have no amends to make and no opportunity
to be braver than your life.*
–Brené Brown

Dealing with Regrets

I believe in my core that if you were to ask everyone who has lost someone close if they ever felt a degree of regret over the loss, they would admit that they did. The regret itself may or may not be reasonable or logical, but it exists. It's just a silent feeling. I've always raised my boys believing that feelings are neither right nor wrong—they just are. I also raised them to live without regrets. Life was meant to be experienced to its fullest.

During the immediate loss, I remember going through the "if onlys." If only Jordan had decided to come down to Florida for Christmas, he'd be alive. If only I had known he was using drugs, I could have saved him. Did I miss something right in front of me that would have prevented this catastrophic event in our lives? Was I a bad mother? Why couldn't he trust me enough to confide in me so that I could have helped him? Do the onlookers think I was deliberately oblivious? The questions are truly endless.

During immediate grief, regrets penetrate nearly every self-talk discussion you have. It's a difficult emotion to toggle because it requires you to admit to weakness, irresponsibility, and perhaps blame. It could be the cornerstone to eroding your belief system as a whole. The cascading of self-doubt is endless. I remember dwelling on regret for many months before I could even articulate the feeling. When I was able to give it a voice, I could only admit it to my husband. Never anyone else. The shame is incredible. It's important to know it can and does exist at some level.

As a parent, you should be able to detect problems with your children innately. As a mom especially, we have the instinct or intuition to know how our kids truly are doing. Yet in this particular situation, my instinct was turned off. The questions asking "Why?" surface without any resolution. I honestly felt as if I'd dropped the ball. His death was my fault.

Regret may be leaked out to others as well, only to be shut down by listeners. Yet we all need to realize that regrets are *real*. They need to be talked through and, to a degree, honored. Looking back, giving it a voice was part of the healing process for me. I had immense regrets about not seeing that my son had a problem and not fixing it. I beat myself up relentlessly for not catching the problem and doing something about. It took time to work through. Surprisingly, it still pops through my mind in my weaker moments.

I heard a great talk years later that put things into better perspective. The speaker asked: Why do we think we are so instrumental in folks' lives, their choices and their destinies? What gives us that power over others that through one intervention by us, we'd have such a revolutionary impact? Why do we think we have the gift to change lives with mere chronology of events and timing? The speech continued to focus on the concept of decision making and free will (by others). It was free will that had this power to influence—not us as the bystander. It was Jordan's choice to take the drug that night, for whatever reason, and accidentally end his life. Granted, we could have changed the event's timing perhaps, but the ultimate result remained in Jordan's hands. If not now, it would have for sure been later.

I also remember bystanders asking me, *"You didn't know he was on drugs?"* While I understand that such questions come from a knee-jerk-reaction place, know that these types of questions trigger the guilt and regrets already laced throughout my cells. The lesson I have learned is to not ask anything that could potentially trigger this destructive emotion of regret. Yes, I say destructive because regrets don't help the healing. They hinder.

Dealing with Regrets

There is another aspect to the grief journey and regret that often enters the picture. It is around karma and, perhaps linked to that, the concept of punishment. Before Jordan, I thought I totally understood life's balance around karma. I was not at all a saint, but anyone who knew me would assuredly say I was a good person. I firmly believed that if you give kindness and "good" to the world, the world would reciprocate. Good becomes good—a seemingly easy concept, I thought. I was naturally wired to be kindhearted so karma would follow suit and give me a good life. I brought up my boys to believe this as well. *Then December 2014 happened.*

Processing such a profound loss naturally takes you into a place of profound uncertainty. Everything that you once believed is challenged. *Everything.* Every relationship you have is challenged, and you restart, learning your new life. You do not feel wise in any aspect of your life. You do not feel even safe! You are back to square one—it's all different. This is counterintuitive because fresh grievers are yearning to know when things will return to normal. The sooner they realize that their lives need to ebb and flow with the circumstances to reinvent themselves, the better the grieving will process. For those who don't like change, it will be very difficult.

I was processing the "Why" to such a deep degree that it made me unsure of nearly everything in my life as I had come to know it to be. It wasn't fair. It wasn't deserved. It wasn't at all balanced. It totally went against everything I had come to believe in the fiber of my being for so many years. The shock of what happened led to questioning everything I was comfortable in knowing and essentially returning to the basics. Looking back on this phenomenon, it was as if I had lost all memory and needed to build the new foundation for my belief system.

While I am not trained in psychology, I did gain an understanding why folks who deeply grieve lose interest in their career, their spouse, and their hobbies. I suspect it is linked to this evolvement into a new outlook on life. The priorities have shifted, friends shift, and focus is altered. This is the time when the griever feels they are "losing it" and may need help. But what if the griever knew that this was a possibility and they could embrace it with eyes wide open? Yes, they are *losing it,* but it's to get to the new normal.

Grief opens a place in our hearts that we never knew could hurt so profoundly but also opens this same place to a love we never imagined possible.
–Unknown

Family Dynamics with Grieving

When a family grieves, it essentially dissolves for a while. I can guess that it's possible to split permanently depending on the degree of loss, the family health prior to the event, and role that individual may have held within the family tribe. Prior to Jordan dying, our family had a special cadence of strong personalities, outrageous humor, competition, and drive. Conversations were spirited and highly dynamic in a consistently respectful manner. We had our own language and nicknames, memory tags, and traditions. Our family was undeniably close and weirdly predictable. The family home was a place to be sheltered from the hardships of the outside world at all times. The boys knew that they could walk through our doors and be protected, healed, and (especially) loved. Whatever was said at family dinners stayed at family dinners, and we all had each other's back.

Gary and I were married in 1979 against the passionate opposition of my parents and some friends. "You are clearly direct opposites." "It simply won't work." Yet when I first met Gary, it was love at first sight and, fast-forward to today, it remains strong. He's my yin to my yang. I think that the fact we are so opposite complements our weaknesses and makes us a force to be reckoned with. He's my heartbeat, best friend, my rock, and my person.

When loving parents lose a child, you often hear that the marriage suffers. I totally understand why, now. What isn't said is that the loss hitting both parents actually removes them from the role you need desperately in your life to successfully grieve. Why? Because they are emotionally unavailable for however long it takes to dig out of the cavernous pain.

Gary has always been the one to protect and shield me from any harm or risk of harm. He is, by definition, a fixer. He's always had one eye on me to ensure I'm all right, even under the best and most ordinary of circumstances. I've never asked him to do this. It's just in his DNA to care for me in any way possible. I, in turn, have always been his sounding board, his conscience, and his voice of perspective. I also have a keen creative side that helps him fine-tune many of his projects. When he had hard times, I naturally picked up the load—just as he would for me. We didn't need to ask each other—we just jumped in. Together, we

Family Dynamics with Grieving

have this dynamic to balance what is needed to get things done. That all changed in December.

During the early weeks, Gary was the strong one. He needed to take care of not only me, but also Justin, TJ, and Kate. He had to ensure we were all right before he tended to himself. What I learned later is that Gary would grieve alone so as not to inflict more sorrow upon any of us. What we saw, however, was a man who didn't seem to demonstrate anguish. *Did he hurt as much as we did?* He also returned to work a week after Jordan passed. I was astonished that he could do that! He'd go in the den, take calls from his colleagues, accept their condolences as if he was confirming an order, and proceed with the business at hand. *Did he feel anything?*

I was unable to return to work for almost three weeks. Looking back, that was too soon! While my employer had a three-day bereavement benefit, my managers were kind enough to let me take as long as I needed. I chose to remain at home to try to re-center, without much success. My work had my colleagues there, and I genuinely missed them. They, too, were family. So, I did return when I believed it was the right time. It wasn't.

What they don't tell you is that when you lose someone like a child or perhaps your spouse, folks simply don't know what to say at work. The once-casual banter that you crave has evaporated. They look at you differently and you can tell that they don't know what to say for fear of saying the wrong thing.

I would look forward to coming back home to Gary, having dinner in sullen, peaceful silence, which provided us comfort. I was with someone who knew my pain. I was in a safe place. No masks were needed. We were able to re-center each other to a degree and be able to resume our life as we knew it. We were grappling to return to normal. It didn't seem right, though.

There was an abyss that existed between Gary and me that was unexplainable. Our connection became frail as it was starved of its levity, affection, and warmth. The emotional vacancy was palpable. He couldn't fix me, and I couldn't fix him. Our relationship became mechanical and purposely careful as not to create more pain in each other. I didn't have my best friend to lean on. He didn't have me. Our mutual synergy was now a polite vacuum. Ironically, this was because we hurt so much inside and kept thinking of ways how not to create more pain for the other person!

The mindset had become that if I had actually told Gary how dark I felt inside, it wasn't fair to him to contend with my emotions when he had to work through his own. By protecting each other with silence with the best intentions, we created a distance that continually grew and eventually eroded our relationship. This resulted in isolation and loneliness, even though prior to losing Jordan, our marriage relationship was strong and predictable.

I believe that it wasn't for several months after Jordan passed that I came to feel the loneliness being together. To be candid, it scared me. I loved Gary with all my being, and now, with this emotional interloper in our marriage, I was unsure if we'd ever be able to rebound from the distance. This is probably the reason why marriages do suffer after the loss of a child.

I remember a poignant moment when I was in bed, thinking of Jordan. I was obsessed that I was losing the memory of Jordan's voice. I was silently distraught. I don't remember why I felt the compulsion to find a picture of him at that late hour, but I did. I got out of bed, rifled through our photo drawer in the living room, when Gary came up behind me, hearing me whimper. It was controlled crying. He asked me what I was doing, and I blurted out, *"I'm looking for his picture! I am forgetting things about him and need to remember. I can't even remember his voice!"* At that profound moment, I lost control of my bladder. My dear husband saw my utter collapse, scooped me up, help me change out of my clothes, cleaned up the soiled floor, and held me tight in bed until I fell asleep. That was the breakthrough of our silence. From that point, our communication shifted toward the better. *What if that moment had never happened?*

We needed to address the isolation we felt together head-on, and that was just another painful element that needed to be identified on this journey. It's not easy to tell your significant other that they are not helping you or you are helping them. You truly risk the chance that the other will say it's too hard to work on. That they are already emotionally depleted and to ask more of them now is unrealistic. Yet to live in the "polite rhythm" a day longer couldn't happen.

Approximately six months after Jordan left us, I was driving Gary to the airport on my way to work. It's something we did quite often, as his job took him out of town often. He was beginning to get back into the full demands of his sales position, and from all appearances his life was business as usual.

I can't tell you why, but, for whatever reason, during our twenty-minute ride, Gary stated that he felt I was quieter than normal that early morning. Because I was so emotionally drained, it all poured out at that moment. I told him that I was not in a good place, I wanted the relentless pain to stop, and that I wanted to kill myself. He said nothing for about five minutes, as I began to inwardly get angry. Why did I divulge that vulnerable feeling if he obviously didn't care! What seemed to be an eternity later, he calmly asked if I had a plan. I offered that I did. Again, silence.

We pulled up to the airport, and he got out with the parting words that I had until noon that day to ask work for more time off. He'd be home later that evening and we'd figure it all out then. For now, he needed to go. I was hurt that work seemed to take priority over my vulnerable admission, but at that same time, I didn't really care. I drove to work. Within ten minutes of getting to my office, my boss showed up, closed the door, and promptly asked me how I was doing. I told him that I needed more time at home, at which he readily approved. He made sure I left immediately and assured me that he'd take care of whatever was needed for whatever amount of time I needed. It wasn't until later that day that I was able to connect the dots: Gary had entered the airport doors, called my boss, and made arrangements for me (again) to be safe until he came home several hours later. There was a silent network of folks shepherding me to get me help.

When Gary got home that afternoon, I admitted that I needed to check myself into a place to prevent me from self-harm. I am a nurse. I know the criteria to self-admit for care. It scared me tremendously admitting that, but I knew I was not in a good place. That the first tiny glimmer of me digging out. However, that never happened. Gary said he wanted me to first give him the opportunity to help me along with our oldest son, Justin, acknowledging that all of us seemed to be in our cocoon. Because I was ambivalent whether I wanted to still live this so-called life or die, I agreed. I remember

Justin getting on the phone with me that same evening and saying something I will never forget. Justin said *"Ma, pull yourself up!"* I told him I didn't think I could, but he insisted that I needed to do this for him, for TJ, and for Kaiden—and *especially for Gary*.

Our sons were able to share that seeing their normally strong, resilient parents so broken was painfully unbearable to watch. We were a symbol of how life around them was so fragile. They needed their parents now more than ever, and we weren't available. They had to be strong to carry us, which felt foreign. They, too, had the mentality that if they brought their pain to us to talk through, it somehow wasn't fair. Gary and I were doing all that we could to put one foot in front of the other, and the last thing that they wanted to do was burden us. While collectively our family wanted to protect each other, we were strangling the air from each other's bodies to heal. What I learned is that we needed to *lean into the grief* no matter how painful.

I now realize that for our family, we grieved in what was probably a typical, expected way, but it wasn't the way that our family needed. I remember telling Gary to fix the family. I had already lost one son and felt I was losing the others, all because of the emotional isolation. We needed to be a family again as we knew how—not what society expected. We needed to regain a family that resembled when Jordan was with us. We all craved that. It was Gary's task (unfairly assigned) to fix us and get us there. It was another moment where we began to dig ourselves out.

When a family grieves, each member grieves differently. They still feel the same loss, but it's demonstrated in different ways. It was inappropriate for me to think that because Gary went back to work right away, he didn't ache. It was inappropriate to think that because I was the mom, my sons didn't have the same degree of loss as his brothers. Yet it is how I thought for nearly a year. I assumed things versus verifying them. If I had only asked the tough questions and started hard conversations with them, as painful as they would have been, I wouldn't be able to heal. I learned that by going into places that scared and hurt me, and were uncomfortable, they were the keys to me taking back control of my life.

One other aspect of family dynamics pertains to those friends extremely close to you. There are those around us who actually feel the pain as we do. In our case, we had a few friends (couples) who we have known for decades. They saw Jordan as a young boy and felt his loss. Often there are no words to share with each other because the emotions are brutal. It's a pact shared by a lifetime of memories. Today, many years past Jordan's death, these couples still tear up when speaking about him. We cherish them in our lives because they are able to celebrate the wonderful man our son was, with intimate memories, laughter, and joy. It's important to let those people into your lives and allow them to carry you through the tougher days. It's equally just as important to carry them—they will never ask you for this, but they need it. The loss we share binds us for life. Remember this as a collateral gift that lasts a lifetime.

*Time only teaches us to conceal our pain
from others and we learn to grieve
by ourselves.*
−Narin Grewal

Maneuvering to Survive

When someone close to you passes away, it kicks the wind from your body. For me, it was a blow akin to a full football team pummeling me to the ground as if to score a point. The grief levels that follow are not only foreign but uncomfortable, and they shift every ounce of your mental equilibrium. Grief takes you into the recesses of your mind that you never thought existed. You are mechanically functional, but your mind sweeps you to a place of cloudiness, pain, and with no sense of present time. I was stuck in the past wearing concrete boots as it pertained to Jordan. Yet to survive, you need to dig yourself back to present-day reality, which greets you with relentless pain, perhaps regret and loss as well. Folks never tell you of the immediate steps for a fresh loss, so I will give you my perception.

The Autopsy

As a mother, you are naturally wired to ensure that no harm ever comes to your child. Every bump, bruise, and cut is felt by the mother with an immediate mission to alleviate, soothe, and cure. To know that your son has been taken for autopsy is immensely counterintuitive to your motherly instincts. Yet by law, in New York State, for any death occurring in a suspicious, unusual, or unexplained manner, this is a requirement. This is especially true with a young death. It was also our only recourse for getting answers about his final moments.

As a nurse, I knew what any good autopsy included. I knew that my precious son would be taken to a cold examining room; his bones severed meticulously with a bone saw; his organs removed, weighed, and placed onto a stainless table, resulting in a reasonable determination of the actual cause of death. We would have answers. However, the report with answers to our questions would take six to nine months to process. His lifeless body would be put back together in a quick, expedient fashion like putting together a Build-A-Bear. Then his lifeless body would be returned to us. I saw his serous fluid seep from the skull incision onto the casket pillow. *To me, this had to be the worst part of losing a child.*

Practicalities

After the funeral comes the logistics of emptying his home and preparing it for sale, finding suitable homes for his two dogs, speaking with attorneys to get the necessary documents to process these milestones, and emptying his closet. Our devastated daughter-in-law could barely maintain a semblance of a normal routine for our two-year-old grandson, so we needed to all step in and do what we could to help her. The closet was the hardest part because his clothes smelled of Jordan. He had a smell of cologne, fresh soap, and cigarettes. All of his personal items carried this aroma, which simultaneously put band aids on my heart while comforting my soul. For brief aromatic moments, he was back with me. *This now had to be the hardest part of the nightmare we're in.*

Living Numbly

I was a vibrant senior executive at a budding medical organization prior to Jordan's death. I was sharp, focused, creative, and energetic. I remember thinking in early 2014 that I felt I was at the pinnacle of my career I'd worked so hard to achieve. When you lose someone so close, that punch in the gut banishes most of the survivor's attributes. My personality shifted, my priorities were wistful, and I felt as if I was medicated with a numbing drug minute after minute. Amazingly, I was able to go through the motions at work, but my heart was not healed enough to feel its drive. Like ripples circling when a rock is tossed in a pond, this family's fallout was immeasurable. It was relentless. We all were numb but didn't know how to traverse it. We felt comfortable being in this trap but knew we needed to come back to a fully engaged reality.

You Are Part of The Club

I heard this phrase more than I care to recount during my journey. There are also special cards or trinkets folks will include in their condolence cards! A membership card, really? Frankly, it irritated me. This isn't a Club. It's a process in life. We all will sustain loss at some point in our lives. Granted, losing a child is almost unimaginable but so is losing a spouse or a parent or a partner. So why have the concept of a special segregated and unique tribe? It's not anything of status, specialness or elite living. This is simply what happened to someone which will most likely be experienced by someone else next year. My advice to those reading this book is to eliminate this Club mentality from your vernacular because you risk the possibility of the message being lost. I would recommend that you simply acknowledge the pain of the loss they feel. It's that simple.

The Firsts

After you've had some time to study the cards that life has given you, there comes random firsts. These are the first holidays, anniversaries, birthdays, and the first anything that could commemorate a memory. There is no guidebook instructing you how to be during these times. I also need to acknowledge that folks need to decide for themselves what makes sense to do—for them. For our family, we decided to embrace these firsts, dedicating appropriate attention to each of them in whatever fitting way we could. It was important for us as a family to celebrate Jordan, as he still remains part of this family. He's just not with us physically any longer.

We celebrate his birthday every year by having his favorite dinner and doing a toast. We also share stories during the meal. It's typically lighthearted and uplifting, yet deep in our individual souls, we ache. It's the way Jordan would insist on us carrying on. We actually find ourselves referencing him on a multitude of occasions throughout the year. All have that sharp humor resulting in laughter.

Because the anniversary of his death is Christmas, we purposefully do not extend our respects. We are entitled to a festive holiday with family. It's healthy. What we typically do is go to his gravesite and say our tributes. Throughout the anniversary, however, one can't avoid the "X number of years ago at this time . . ." recollections. We admit that we recount the final moments, last conversations, and details leading up to this journey privately in our tireless minds. I feel that it will never leave us, and to a degree, perhaps it's normal to do. I don't feel, as humans, that it's able to be turned off. We know we'll go there in our thoughts, relive and process the etched moments, and learn to put them away until the next milestone returns. This is part of the grief package that is now part of me. This isn't to say that gravesite visits are natural for others. My sons and husband don't frequent his plot as routinely as I do because they don't *need to*. Jordan simply is with them in his own way. I have come to respect that because grief is spelled differently for everyone.

The Focus of Attention

What is a natural by-product of loss is becoming the center of attention in group gatherings. Death is uncomfortable for most to embrace. It's as if a shroud has been draped over the survivor, and others are reluctant to approach. No one will admit it, but the survivor has been stigmatized at some level. It is driven by the onlookers' perceptions and experiences with death. Many do not know what to say. It's a taboo subject and feared instinctively by many.

I am naturally shy. Attention was not something I coveted. When I would enter a group, the looks by well-meaning participants reeked of pity. I totally get it now, looking back, but while experiencing it live, it was not helpful. I wanted to get up and scream, *"I'm okay. I'm the same person I was prior to Jordan's death, and I won't break!"* But was I really? Instead, I was relentlessly polite because I knew they were equally uncomfortable.

The lesson this experience taught me was to approach other survivors with the dignity and strength they sorely need. I am very conscious of not emitting any suggestion of pity. I do sympathize and empathize, but pity is different. It's feeling bad for that other person with a slight dash of shame or embarrassment. Instead, I have learned to approach a survivor with open conversations of their loss but in a reflective, positive fashion. I also encourage a hug if the griever is receptive. Hugging is like the reset button for your cable television. There's a feeling of release for that person, which removes any awkwardness. I let them know that I understand and am willing to be present for them and listen. They are experiencing one of life's toughest challenges, and I want them to know I'm simply there with them—mostly to listen, which they need so desperately.

Business as Usual

While we are on the topic of post-death idiosyncrasies, there's the other phenomenon that occurs when your social circle or work group expects you to return to business as usual. Nothing in a survivor's life remains usual any longer. It's all been affected at some degree. What all parties need to realize is that there is a need to redefine what that "usual" will now be or look like. There's a mix of gingerly approaching the griever while expecting that the griever will be as alert, focused, and driven as before. None of that is accurate.

My advice on this matter is to conduct open conversations with the survivor to see what the expectations are now. How will that work for all parties, and what can each party do to reaffirm previous commitments and relationships? Openly discuss how the dynamics have or need to change. An employer has every right to expect the job to be done if his/her employee is a survivor—but how that will look may or may not fit within that organizational model and current demands. There needs to be a mutual realignment and commitment for this to remain healthy and productive. This holds true as well for relationships outside of work. By having that conversation, the griever is forced to be introspective as to how he/she really is at that juncture and honest as to what his/her capabilities can be. The employee owes that to the employer just as much as the employer needs to work with the employee. Three days of bereavement is not enough.

Seeking Help

I have walked in struggling shoes and know what red flags I was demonstrating of my internal turmoil. I can honestly tell you that I asked myself at least a hundred times, *"Is this normal?"* I was in foreign territory maneuvering this pain and felt alone and isolated. The only "person" I had available that knew the pulse of where I actually was, was me. Others around me appeared to be handling things better than I was. This actually created an illusion of how I was supposed to be. Deep down, I knew I was immensely broken and sick. I wanted to die.

I was clinical enough to know that my thoughts were approaching that dangerous line of stability versus precarious. If pushed across that line, it would be easy for me to end my life. I didn't want to live with the pain any longer. I was exhausted, ate poorly, lacked energy, and mentally escaped reality as much as possible. I didn't drink or use drugs and was not interested in starting. I was fortunate enough to know the tipping point and give those feelings a voice. I am sure others don't recognize the demons. They may succumb. I simply was lucky. Looking back, I was fine-tuning my ability to be self-aware. I also recognize that there may be others feeling the turmoil who might not have the supports around them to pull them back up from the darkness. There are wonderful resources available such as those offered by the Suicide Prevention Center webpage (https://suicidepreventionlifeline.org/). The key point to be made is to acknowledge the pain and ask for help.

My recommendation as a survivor is to be real with yourself. Pay attention to the self-harm thoughts. Where does your mind travel when allowed? What do you think about at two in the morning when you can't sleep? Do you initially think dark thoughts but then readily pull yourself up, or do you dwell and anguish with them over long periods of time? Are you letting your body deteriorate? You need to constantly take a survey of these things and have a plan on how you will address them.

When I began to want to actively commit suicide, I became very withdrawn and unusually quiet. I became more organized so as not to burden my family with where things might be that they would need. We have a sheet near my desk with all the passwords and accounts. That was up to date. I felt a flatness of emotion—not as dark but not as positive, either. Simply level and steady, like a machine. These were red flags!

Then the hard part comes when you need to verbalize the tipping point to your loved ones or a professional. You need to give what you are a voice. Own it. Sure, it's humbling, perhaps embarrassing to a degree, but if you don't share what you feel at your core, then you can't get the help you need. This is hard! Most likely THE hardest thing a human can do is to admit weakness, failure, and apathy. With folks around you to carry you through these times, it is possible to come out from under this immensely heavy grief blanket we wear. But you need to speak its truth and let folks in.

I did try a couple of counselors but if I was being honest, it was a waste of time. For me, I needed a counselor that also experienced loss. This isn't a textbook recipe you are given to dig out from this pit. You need to be able to share the myriad emotions to someone who truly *"gets it."* Thankfully, our family did find the most perfect therapist and I attribute that to the fact that he, too, experienced a profound loss. When we shared, it was immediately understood—that is what you need to find with a professional.

It is kind of shocking when your world falls to pieces and everything and everyone around you carries on with life. How can the birds continue to sing? How can people carry on loving life? It is like you have become frozen in time and are now watching life like a movie. As the weeks and months roll by, life becomes more real again but you will never forget that point in time where life stood still.
–Zoe Clark-Coates

When the World Seems to Go On Uninterrupted

It's been six years since our son Jordan passed away. Throughout the years, we would tell our daughter-in-law that when the time was right, she needed to move on and begin a new life with a man whom she would love. We earnestly meant these words. Kate was only twenty-six when she lost her husband. Since then, she's been raising our grandson Kaiden while working full-time as a Nurse Practitioner in a local hospital. Parenting was a natural for Kate because she seemed to execute the motherhood challenges with grace, fortitude, and resiliency. In many ways,

I admire her for her ability to do all that she was able to do.

Kate's incredibly beautiful. Her natural blond beauty is the type that might have women staring at times. She definitely has "the package" for any deserving man. She is intelligent, loyal, and resourceful. It was just a matter of time before someone would find her gifts as treasures and sweep her off her feet. We would be there to support her every step of the way. Yet she was steadfast in telling us that she was simply not interested in dating, let alone getting married again. Jordan was her self-professed soul mate, and that would last a lifetime for her.

This past year, Kate announced that she was getting married to a man who is very deserving of her and Kaiden. After we met him, I let Kate know that we could not have hand-picked a better man for her! The important aspect was that he was amazingly kind and patient with our grandson. Fast-forward to the other day when they announced they would wed; it was wonderful news to hear. Yet after it had time to penetrate my reality, it was clear that it also stung for some reason. It did feel as if Jordan had been replaced, and she could experience a fresh new beginning. I needed to focus on the fact that this was tremendously great news for her. However, it carried with it some sadness, because at some level our son was further away from the dynamics of Kate and Kaiden.

He was now a chapter in their lives to be continued on by the creation of a new family.

One aspect of loss is that there is no reversing the perpetual feelings of the "if onlys"—especially for a parent. While we are delighted with Kate's new chapter, our loss of our child can never be "replaced." There are no new beginnings, fresh starts, or refreshes. The loss will be the same now as it was six years ago, as it will be six years from now. This dichotomy in grief is a very real challenge for the survivor to process. How come life "goes on" as it does? How is it possible that we feel the world crashing down around us, yet the real world continues on as business as usual? In a very illogical sense, life should be permanently marred by the profound loss! Yet no matter what, most of what we knew to be real remains constant.

When Kate mentioned she would be married, it then added what I call "cascading thoughts." How will it work when her new husband incorporates his daughter from a previous marriage into the family dynamics? What is the relationship to us should Kate have another child with her new husband? Kaiden will inherit new grandparents, so are we further removed? What are the rules for speaking of Jordan when her husband is with us? Will he adopt Kaiden and have him assume his surname? With reasonable thinking, one could simply define these new dynamics early on to decipher what everyone wants to see. I totally do understand that this is the most mature strategy. However, the emotional side of me still creates scenarios that seem unsolvable and most assuredly to my disadvantage. That is what grief does—it creates havoc with normal, easy-to-solve situations with communication.

I share this phenomenon with you only as a beacon for it being a normal yet convoluted scenario to process. I am an advocate that it all does work out as it needs to be in the end. I try not to be entangled along the way on the path to that ultimate end. However, it's hard not knowing, and fearing the results. As I mentioned to a close friend this week, it gets so tiring always having to process feelings—which others who have not lost don't need to endure. It is during times like these that the weight of the rocks in the permanently stitched backpack on my body wants to pull me down, yet again.

It is at times like these that I need to consciously remember how I traversed the harder moments as best as I was able and came out stronger and more resilient. When you are coping with a loss, you become emotionally scarred to a degree. Thoughts can be exaggerated and unreasonable. Yet they exist and need to be handled in as healthy a way as they can at that point in the grief journey. Some days will be too difficult to manage, but there's always a tomorrow that can let me, once again, embrace, accept, and move on. With each step forward, I feel stronger.

I'm not perfect. I'll annoy you, piss you off and say the dumbest of things always at the worst of times. But you will never find anyone more loyal to love you through the darkest of hours because I care enough to relentlessly stay by your side.
–Cheri A. Copie

Dumb Things People Say

When you lose someone you love, admittedly it's easy to become irritated with things people say. I took offense to many things immediately after losing my son. My feelings were raw. It wasn't until nearly a year or so later that I was able to clearly see the dynamics at play.

As a rule, humans don't know what the right thing is to say in some situations. Yet the compulsion to say something is undeniable. In my opinion, it originates from our human need to comfort, be empathetic, and basically be kind. However, when someone is in pain from loss, the formula for what to say is cloudy.

When we lost our son Jordan, I was amazed at the total lack of empathy that I perceived. Years now down the road, I have come to the conclusion that most of these folks were doing their best at trying to soothe or make me feel better. It was almost as if they were trying to give me a "healthier perspective," because from their lens, they saw that I was drowning in the dark grips of sadness and despair. In essence, they were trying to show me love, albeit clumsily and often to a degree hurtful.

What follows now are examples of what was said, descriptions on how it made me feel, and what now I choose to believe was the intent. It is only now, years hence, that I have the "healthier perspective." It's important to note that in none of these instances did the communicator mean ill will.

"God only gives you things that you can handle."

In a later chapter, I get into how grieving affects faith. So, for now, I will simply touch the surface of this comment. If you don't take anything else away from reading my words, please appreciate the corrosive nature of telling someone in sorrow that God only gives them what they can handle. *I choose to believe* that the speaker meant well. However, there is absolutely no value in telling a grieving person this statement. The listener is thinking, *"So if I was inadequate and weak, my child would still be living?"* That makes no logical sense whatsoever. What is indirectly being communicated is that God is a testing being and challenges only certain people selectively to grow in some obscure way. The griever cannot take any solace from this concept because it can't adequately explain their innermost question, which bubbled up during the first few days of the loss. *"Why me?"*

"Well, you have other kids, right?"

I am perplexed at a common question and response. If I choose to be vulnerable enough with someone disclosing that I lost my son, on a significant number of times, folks will react by reminding me that I have other children. As if to diminish the loss because there's more in my mother/ child bucket. I often want to snap back by replying, *"You are so right! I'm so glad that Jordan wasn't my only son because then it would definitely hurt!"* Even while writing this, I don't seem to come to terms why that response would enter the picture! If I were to wave a magic wand to eliminate DTPS (dumb things people say), it would be to have the listener refrain from even saying anything like that because there sincerely is no benefit, purpose, or positive outcome that could result.

"Everything happens for a reason."

If I were to poll those who grieve, I would venture to conclude that they would all say that this phrase is

Dumb Things People Say

terribly overused. To those wracked in grief and pain, there is no reason that could possibly justify the deep agony of loss. It's been nearly six years without my son, and to this very moment, there is no reason that became clear to any of us. More important, what the cantor is doing is dismissing the authentic feelings of loss. It's another way of saying to us to be grateful or accepting. Grief is a process that needs to be executed in whatever fashion or path it takes the victim. The most important thing a bystander can do is simply acknowledge the loss, allow the grieving party to feel its sting, and guide them along this path toward a healthy acceptance (if that's even possible).

I remember a tragic event in Upstate New York several years back when a crazed man entered an Amish school and killed several innocent children. It devastated their community along with the many area and state residents who felt their pain. The Amish community immediately forgave the perpetrator, which brought amazement to the entire area! They were resolute and perhaps subscribers to the theory that all happens for a reason. However, their faith was so abundantly strong that it surpassed mainstream humanness. This was the exception for sure. To this day, I am humbled that they can forgive and accept the circumstances at play—especially when I feel their same pain. I point out this example to simply demonstrate that there may be some proponents of everything having a reason. But it's rare. I would suggest to well-meaning comforters to refrain from pushing this theory unless the griever offers this as an explanation.

"Time will heal."

As I've shared before, my husband and I often reach out to other parents who have lost children in hopes of providing a "walking in your shoes" perspective. We do this because it lends the grievers another supporting resource. Some can use the perspective because it fully resonates. Others can't relate because their situation is unique. In any case, Gary and I accept where they are in whatever capacity they need.

One question that arises within the first five minutes of conversation is: *"When will things return to normal?"* Gary and I are pragmatic and always reply: "Never." In our opinion, they have a new normal. What follows typically is the parent recounting how folks tell them time will heal. I would love to say that losing someone eventually fades, but it doesn't. Time doesn't heal. It doesn't take away the transient moments where you are fine one moment then see something that reminds you of your loved one and puts you back into the same blubbering human who wants to have just a few more moments with their loved one.

Time doesn't heal. It's a fact. But what time does afford is the ability to better *handle* the loss. The raw emotions now become more patterned and manageable—the angst is still there, but we're better able to control it from leaking outside of our innermost being. I often say that over time, we are stronger every day from the rigors of having to carry this immense backpack of rocks everywhere—much like someone who works out at the gym every day. Our coping muscles have strengthened.

A well-meaning friend offering "time" as a healer risks giving the griever false hope—that things will eventually "*get back to normal.*" However, when the grieving person doesn't get back to a place of normal, they may feel like they are stuck or not healing as they should. What I have learned is that folks need to travel the grief path at their own authentic pace, modality, and direction. The healing that takes place is akin to a broken bone that was never properly aligned and casted, and so has reformed into a new shape. The new normal.

"Shouldn't you be over it by now?"

I think this was the most common statement I heard, yet the most damaging. What the speaker is implying is that the grief journey the person is on is not healthy. There's something wrong. Maybe they should be doing more. It also makes the griever self-conscious because they wonder how they appear to others if that comment is merited.

As with anyone who journeys grief, I come from my own experience. But I can tell you that when most grievers hear this, it hurts them. I know because they often share this with me. The griever essentially feels shut down by their community or workplace and automatically wants to work on getting better—not because it feels natural but because they don't want to appear more devastated than they genuinely are. They feel like their unique grief path is not healthy compared with social norms.

When I heard this (which actually came from people in my workplace on several occasions), I felt oddly insulted and defeated. I was putting forth the very best public effort I was able to muster each and every day and was being told: it's not enough. I can share with you now that someone who deeply grieves never will *"get over it."* There's no end with the unfinished love you had for the departed. It's still there in their lives—except now it is permeated with a jacket of profound loss. What the griever needs to try to achieve is to be able to *get through it*.

I think back to the days of my darkest despair when my wise therapist Mark told me to go *into the grief*. He said that I needed to pass through the pain, the regrets, and the utter loss to get out to the other side. I've never fully understood what constitutes the "other side," and today I still am unable to articulate what that actually is. But I do know that the feelings I was able to tap into on the "other side" felt healthier and less of a burden to carry. It's as if a stream of sunshine would flash into a dark room and onto my pain, lessening the sting.

I always have to come back to why folks might say what they say, however. I believe when they say, "When are you able to get over this?" they are actually trying to see when you will return to normal and regain the relationship you once had with *them*. They want to help the griever and the only (uneducated) way to do that is to drive the griever in the direction of returning to the days of pre-loss. While these words, when spoken, hurt the receiver to the core, *I choose to believe* that it most likely comes from a caring place.

"I know how you feel because I lost my grandma recently."

It always provided a bit of silent comic relief to me when someone would awkwardly equate our loss with the loss of their grandparent or great uncle. Losing an elderly grandparent who'd had the ability to live a lifetime of experiences just couldn't compare with losing someone whose life was shortened. You expect to lose your grandparents. You also expect to lose your parents during your adulthood. You even expect to lose your spouse someday, although way down the road. You don't expect to lose someone younger than yourself that you were assigned to protect as your child. It simply feels unnatural. Again, when I heard this, it minimized the feelings I felt. Granted, there are losses of others in our life that can rip your heart out with intense grief . I am the first to state that no one can judge the pain a griever feels. The point being made is that losing a child is incredibly unnatural to process.

It eventually left me feeling angry at those who would say this. It wasn't until maybe year two later that I was able to see that these folks were trying their best to identify. To soothe. To say they understood. Granted, they may not have had full comprehension of my personal grief and anguish, but it was important for them to convey that they cared at some level. I look back on these comments and now smile that someone cared enough to simply say they identified.

"Of all the kids you had, wasn't it best that you lost Jordan?"

Yes, someone did say this to me early on in my grief process. Zinger doesn't even cover the shock. I can't say that I've ever come to terms with this question. To me, it was unfathomable to even try to grasp the message laced with the indifference displayed by the asker. *I choose to believe* that the intention was to point out that Jordan always had difficulty with life. He was the "harder child" to raise, if one were keeping score. If I had to select, wouldn't I choose to eliminate from my life the child with the challenges?

I include this as one of the dumb things—not because I think that it will ever be asked to another soul per se, but because I wanted to highlight the callous types of questions one could pose to the griever. If only the observer would have paused for a millisecond and said to themself, "Is this an uplifting, supportive comment?" the comment could have been withheld. I still remember where it was said as if it were yesterday. It stung so much. By not saying it, the griever could have focused on more pertinent emotions toward healing. It truly all comes down to that, if you think about it, the observer wants to say something to buoy the griever because that's what humans do. If we gate-keep the comments by a simple litmus test of being supportive, kind, necessary, uplifting, etc., wouldn't that make such a wonderful difference? Just food for thought.

Every struggle in your life will become a story someday. It will either be a story about how you got stronger and persevered or a story about why you gave up. You can't always choose your struggles, but you can choose which story becomes true.
—Dave Willis

Redefining Core Family Relationships

Marital

What you don't ever hear about is the interesting phenomenon that occurs when a couple grieves. I have the fortuitous situation to be married to my best friend. When I met Gary in 1977, it was love at first sight. (It wasn't for him, but I guess I grew on him.) We've been married decades now. When Jordan passed, we'd been married just past thirty-five years. Marriage is hard. It's a lot of work and yet the joy of knowing you have someone who is there next to you, supporting you, is glorious. We have had a lifetime of ups and downs, but nothing prepared us for the day we received the horrible call.

When we grieved, we each lost access to our best friend. He was always my rock and my foundation. Poof, it vanished in a second of time. We had to maneuver the grief storm alone. There was no energy to spare in either one of us to soothe or comfort. If we'd had any stamina, we'd for sure have given it to our sons.

Couples truly grieve differently. Gary jumped back into work within ten days of burying our son. I could barely function. I was paralyzed with grief, loss, regrets, shock, and failure (yes, failure). We were on different paths of recovery. Gary has a remarkable way to compartmentalize situations so as to focus on the task at hand. I marvel at this skill because it allows the person to have eternal focus and control. Being his direct opposite, it's safe to say my way to process is to scramble things altogether in a pot and try to sort it out one by one. My loss bled into everything I tried to do. That's just how I am wired.

I remember a few months after losing Jordan that we decided to go to Miami—just to get away from our condo for a couple nights. It would be a therapeutic weekend of sun, time with each other, and essentially an escape. We had planned this weekend prior to losing Jordan, because there was a concert there, and we'd already purchased tickets.

What happened that second night we were away was that the grief and regret and numbness took over me and made my emotions nothing shy of raw. It was much like a fresh skin burn. Somehow during our time together, I found myself *apologizing* to Gary for being so depressed. He stoically replied to me: *"That's okay. Take the time you need. You don't need to apologize."* If I'm being honest, that reply struck me as being odd—was he "over it"? Why wasn't he feeling the same emotions as me? Gary did help me through my feelings that weekend, and I will be eternally grateful. It was probably the first time he was able to verbalize where he was at during this journey, albeit awkwardly. Yet I judged him at that time. I believed that he was being coldly trite to the death of our son. Little did I know, he was broken inside but didn't want me to take that emotion on, since I was so fragile. In his mind, he needed to be strong.

After months of therapy, I realized that every one of our nuclear family members grieve—but they demonstrate it differently. The feelings of loss are there but maybe not in the form we expect. I share this with you to demonstrate that at many levels, humans are judged by our outside behaviors. Yet we need to step back and explore what lies under the covers. Maybe it comes down to just not assuming and rather asking the right questions, as difficult as it might feel to do.

Through the passing of time, what results between couples is a common bond that can't be broken. Gary is the only person who feels the same loss as me and vice versa. We also share a lifetime event that will be our absolute worst. Nothing else in the future will compare or be more challenging. We've paid our dues.

Today, our marriage is impenetrable. We are aligned with our values, our priorities, and the definition of what really matters. The collateral beauty of this situation resulted in a healthier marriage. I love my spouse more today than I did prior to 2014.

The message to those grieving is to try to lean into each other whenever possible. It may feel off-balance or possibly fake. But your partner needs this emotionally. Rely on each other's instincts to help each other. Grow together in the same direction with deeper roots and mightier branches. Listen to each other, whatever feelings are shared. Don't judge. Just accept. Feelings are never right or wrong—they just are. Sometimes just a hug is what is needed. Much like those who came through the wake line—those who had no words told us the most.

Parent-Child

One of my proudest accomplishments is being a mom of three amazing men. Admittedly, at first, I did not want a son, let alone two or three. I grew up in a female-dominated household and knew that to be my norm. But there I was with three, very different, sons.

When we lost Jordan, I found myself totally incapacitated, unable to be the mom I was accustomed to being. I am very hands-on, anticipatory, and reliable to a fault. Instead, I became frozen and introspective. I couldn't bear to see them broken as well. They lost their brother. Their foundation was rocked to the core. The family dynamics had shifted, and everyone was simultaneously juxtaposing for solid footing—whatever that might be.

During the immediate days and weeks after the loss, my sons became the adults and we became the children, to a degree. It was Justin and TJ who led us through the necessary tasks and arrangements. Immediately, they had to shelf their grief and get us to put one foot in front of the other. They took over the arrangements, the communications, blocked us from the public, and

Redefining Core Family Relationships

cared for our daughter-in-law and her two-year-old. They were the ones on the calls. They became the protectors—essentially becoming the parents.

It was not until several months had passed that our boys came up for air and were able to tend to their own pain. As parents, we were able to take back the reins for leading our injured family. Then it became time for us, as parents, to finally tend to our sons. What we realized is that with the passing of just a few months, the grief journey for each of us was now firmly ingrained like a wine stain on a white carpet.

As a mom, I can honestly state that I needed to relearn how to mother—as if I had two new children. They were now different, vulnerable, angry, and shaken. I remember having "polite" conversations with them versus the more casual banter we'd become accustomed to. I hesitated to bring up certain topics for fear of aggravating their well-controlled peace. I would be invading their privacy. It would not be an understatement to say that, for a period of time, I lost my other sons, too. We were all ships in the dark, floating alone. It was uniquely disturbing because the family had evaporated. I wasn't at all sure we'd be able to regain the bond we once had.

There are periods in one's life that are defining moments. I remember standing in our Florida condo pleading, in tears, to my husband to *"do something"* because I felt I was losing the rest of my sons! Looking back, I understand how unfair it was for me to assign the fix to the man I loved so much! How would he know what to do? But Gary is a fixer, and perhaps that was something he'd enjoy doing.

Gary reached out to our primary care doctor to ask for the name of a good family counselor. We were given Mark's name immediately, with the caveat that "he isn't for everyone, but maybe he'll do great with your family." Gary called and scheduled an appointment right away.

When our family went to the first session, Mark asked the questions we were afraid to bring up. He provided the safe arena to speak openly and honestly. We each shared where we were with Jordan's death, and most importantly, articulated what we needed from each other. We learned that the love and affection that we had before Jordan left us was still in each of us. We just didn't know how to communicate with each other any longer and craved for its return.

After months of regular sessions as a family, we not only learned the language needed by each of us, but we also were able to obtain a temperature read as to where each of us was during our grief journey. Today, we still see Mark—but not about Jordan (although now and then quipping about what he'd be saying about the topic). We found the tools learned to enhance our communication were a gift we never wanted to give up. The efforts we expended then have made us a family that is mutually nurturing and safe. I don't think that our family has been as strong since we lost Jordan. Post-collateral beauty.

If I'm being honest, there's also a dynamic that might appear to be irrational—but real. When parent loses a child, they become more protective of the others. Justin always wanted to learn how to pilot a plane. I know this is his dream. Yet because I am so fearful of potentially losing another child, I asked him to refrain. Logic would say that there's no credence with my paranoia, but it's real to me, nonetheless. My goal in life is to someday grant him my blessing and maybe even find him a flight instructor! I'm not there yet, but I always have hope.

Extended Family

There's the dynamic about the aunts, cousins, et cetera, who also have experienced a profound loss. Like the emotions conveyed earlier, the parents and siblings just don't have the energy to comfort. I would surmise that the extended family members feel a degree of abandonment by the nuclear family. There's a disruption of the larger family dynamics.

I remember when we notified the family of Jordan's passing, telling my sister to stay in Boston. For me personally, I knew that if she were in town, I'd be feeling the need to cater to her emotions and looks of pity. That was just me surmising how it would be as her baby sister. After quite a bit of back and forth, she respected my wishes and didn't come to Rochester for the services. Her adult children (Jordan's cousins) came, however. Admittedly, that request I made to my sister was not fair. She had a loss of her nephew, and I was not allowing her to go through the necessary steps for ceremonial closure.

My advice to anyone losing someone is to allow the peripheral parties to do what they feel that they need to do in order to process the loss in a healthy manner. It is the individual's choice and not something to be commandeered by the next of kin. It's equally important to remember that the peripheral relationships have lost. They, too, need ceremonial closure. The only caveat I'd add to that is to be aware when a family member might bring negative energy, drama, or self-attention to the situation and impede the nuclear family's grief. Same holds for subsequent gatherings. If the family gathering cannot be a safe zone for the grieving individuals, come up with another plan. Simply put, this is not time for manners. Instead, it is time for intensive self-care.

It's sad when people you know become people you knew. You can walk right past someone like they were never a big part of your life. How you used to be able to talk for hours and how now, you can barely even look at them.
−Anonymous

Friendship Dynamics

I touched on this earlier in the book when describing the gifts received during the calling hours for the loved one. But what I didn't elaborate on was that during the wake, the griever will be provided cues for friendship stamina. Especially when someone loses a child, the onlookers are horrified. They may not say it outright, but the loss of a child to most people is a parent's worst nightmare.

During the calling hours, folks were immensely kind and thoughtful with their words of encouragement. However, there's a subset of folks who can't speak. The loss hits them deeply as well. All they can do is hug tightly. Fast-forward a few years: those same people will be the ones still grieving.

When we lost Jordan, our circle of friends went quickly askew. I don't know what it was, but there was definitely a shift. More loss actually. When we craved "normalcy" to regain the relationships that existed before our loss, that relationship dynamic changed. What Gary and I saw was an erosion of our social circle. I suspect that folks didn't know how to be with us for fear of bringing us down more that we already were. I've also realized that when we went out with some folks to regain our footing, I was thinking of how petty their problems were or insignificant their complaints were. I would return from seeing them feeling drained and empty. So mutual avoidance took over. What resulted for us was a secondary grieving of our friends. I certainly do not blame them at all but want to point this out as possible collateral loss for the griever.

However, there's an equally noticeable dynamic that occurs. There were folks who truly stepped up, embraced the new reality, carried us through the dark times, allowed us to speak of our loss, cried with us, and have never forgotten that this is part of being our friend. Today, six years later, we have a handful of steadfast, rock solid friends who bless our lives every day. They are our beacon. We are authentic with them, and conversations are meaningful both ways; we share our ups and downs and have had the gift of true friendship, which we otherwise might not have ever experienced. For that, we are grateful beyond words.

There's a third dynamic that develops over time. Death and loss inspire doing things purposefully. We don't waste time or efforts on many things now. We have developed a large circle of acquaintances. These are folks we enjoy seeing at group functions and sharing snippets of time. Yet there will be little to no meaningful conversation. Topics will typically be around places to see, things to own, other people that we know. There is no expectation of them ever asking how we feel or are doing. If it is asked, the "elevator" response will be provided—because that is the arms-length boundary in place for our friendship. These relationships are vital, however. They help the griever re-engage with society and give them opportunities to momentarily drift into a pain-free existence focusing on small talk.

The griever needs this acquaintance role in their lives to sustain within society. The logical tendency is to sequester and lick the wounds endured. But humans need interaction to feel the ground under their numb feet. They need to relearn their societal behaviors and customs all while carrying the backpack of grief-rocks. I say that the circle for acquaintances is large—and that is because the circle of safety to be authentic is now significantly diminished and guarded.

This natural cleansing of relationships is actually a gift.

And once the storm is over, you won't remember how you made it through, how you managed to survive. You won't even be sure, in fact, whether the storm is really over. But one thing is for certain. When you come out of the storm, you won't be the same person who walked in. That is what the storm is all about.
–Haruki Murakami, *Kafka on the Shore*

To Hell and Back–The Mid Stage

Wanting the Pain to Stop

I can't tell you when to expect the moment when the griever wakes up, realizes that it's not a dream, puts on the backpack of rocks he/she needs to continue to carry, and says inwardly that they simply want the pain to stop. Yes, pain. Grief is a silent pain where you feel that your heart truly has broken apart. The pain is in your chest—not your legs, your head, or your stomach—it's in your chest. There's a lot of support for the term "broken heart" because that is exactly where the anguish is located.

I would be lying if I were to announce that I never thought of drinking my pain away or using drugs to ease the pain. Anyone who knows me would be shocked at this statement because I don't enjoy alcohol and have never used hard street drugs. I will admit to smoking pot in earlier days but hated the feeling of losing control. Fast-forward: for me to consider drinking or drugs would be radical. There were fleeting thoughts now and then that crept into my mind. Why? Because I wanted the chronic ache to leave me—even if only for a brief time. I don't honestly know why I never did engage, as I certainly had the access. Today, looking back at my journey, I am proud that I had the strength to refuse.

Seclusion

There's a dynamic that everyone should be aware of for anyone grieving or caring for someone with a loss. Seclusion is a natural reaction—and necessary. What is a conundrum is that society will do everything not to have the griever be alone. I pose to you, the reader, this: When you are sick with the flu, your natural behavior might be to go into bed, pull the covers around your entire body, and be alone. Or when one finds out some very devastating news, the natural reaction is to process, which requires a bit of space and time. Or even as simplistic, when a dog is hurt, you will always see that they go into a corner or under the bed in order to tend to themselves. Isolation, within reason, is healthy for many who grieve. It gives them time to process the new reality and tend to their inner emotions. To not allow a period of seclusion could be immensely detrimental. Why? Because it would not allow the griever time to figure out what he/she needs to go through this experience. They need the venue to process whatever is on their mind.

Earlier I said isolation is healthy—but within reason. There are some who go into this cavernous despair and refuse to dig out. That is when society should try to help the griever. Simultaneously, they will let their physical self-care deteriorate, such as not bathing, not eating, or giving up basic maintenance. Those are the warning signs; no matter how uncomfortable it might be, onlookers need to spring into gentle action.

It was hard for me to go out after Jordan passed. We would be invited to simple social gatherings, and I would decline. If I went out, had any degree of fun or, god forbid, smiled, I felt a disloyalty to my son, who now was dead. How could I ever have any fun going forward? I caught myself laughing but corrected myself as if I were being disingenuous to Jordan's memory. Again, not very reasonable but true. This is the part where the griever needs to actually put themselves into a very unnatural position to re-socialize.

Initially, I hated our outings with friends because the topics were so trivial. I was inwardly thinking: "How can life go on like this when I just lost my son?"

I just wanted to go back home and lick my grieving wounds. Yet Gary and I both knew that that was not an option. We needed to push ourselves to a healthier lifestyle for our kids and each other. This was a very difficult task to assume but incredibly necessary to begin the journey to reinvent our lives.

Going Into the Grief

Best advice ever! The best advice received was the concept of *going into the grief*. If you have but one takeaway from this book, this is immensely important to grasp. It is my opinion that going INTO the grief is the key to a successful grief journey. When I speak to others that feel grief, it is one of the key pieces of information I always leave with them. It's extremely counterintuitive and uncomfortable because the griever already is balancing on shaky, unfamiliar ground. Going into the fire of grief and its cavernous emotions is frankly scary. I would venture to say that some who deeply grieve have given consideration to suicide at some point, just to end the pain. To go into that feared territory risks never coming out safely. There's also the childhood adage that we are to always control our emotions and, at some level, shelve them, to be an adult. By actually relaxing the guarded control means to be vulnerable and submissive to the ache. *Where would this take us?*

As mentioned earlier, I was not the poster child for grief management by any means. I openly admitted to having a plan to kill myself. I simply wanted the memories, the pain, and the emptiness to abate. It was my husband and oldest son who rescued me from that precipice. When I immediately got the help I needed, the therapist said calmly to go into the feelings I was experiencing when they occurred. I needed to forget about controlling the thoughts. There was no rational or irrational in the equation any longer. They were simply thoughts that I needed to face head-on, process, and then put away, hopefully for good.

This was immensely difficult for me because I am innately a control freak. Everything on the outside needed to be perfect. For me to become slave to real-time naked emotions and vulnerability would take every ounce of strength I possessed to successfully do. I did the work that was needed, and, yes, there is light at the end of the abyss! I came away conquering the thoughts I was burying and gained a clearer perspective. To this day, *this* is the most important piece of advice I give anyone dealing with loss.

> *Instead of ignoring loss and trauma, or moving quickly past them, we can choose to slow down, site with each loss, examine it and grieve it. It's better to sink in and experience it head on that to find yourself drowning years later in losses that had no voice.*
> −Christina Hibbert, Psy. D.

Transitional Stage−Maturing and Self-Awareness

Faith, Karma, and Beliefs

I would be remiss not to address a very poignant aspect of an individual during grief—that around faith and beliefs. Pre-loss, I sincerely thought that I had divine understanding about life. I had it all figured out. I was raised Catholic yet was not quite "devout" by the time I hit my thirties. We raised the boys in the faith as well. They even attended Catholic grammar school and a Jesuit high school. Faith was definitely established within the woven fabric of our lives. Most of us believed there was a God for sure, that karma existed, and good things come to good people.

Transitional Stage–Maturing and Self-Awareness

Admittedly, our faith drifted during the years depending on our individual circumstances. But we all had that same foundation. Prior to losing my son, I focused on karma—so for several years, I would do a random act of kindness for someone. I consciously appreciated my fortunate life and family. I can truly say that I never took our family bond for granted. I treasured my three sons immensely, as I felt God knew what he was doing giving me sons to surround me.

When Jordan passed, that entire foundation of what I believed spiritually and psychologically dissipated instantly! *How could this happen to good people? Why would I inherit this nightmare when I lived intentionally good? Where was my God?* I fell away from Church instantaneously. That became difficult because folks around us would say *"I'm praying for you." Ha! Prayers, really?* I couldn't pray for my own comfort lying awake night after night because my faith now didn't make any sense. It certainly blew the concept of karma out of my window as well.

Years later, I still have a cool relationship with God. It's not strong, yet it does linger somewhere in my center. I haven't abandoned it, but I also have not given it recognition. I am honestly not proud to own up to these feelings, but remember, feelings just are. This is an element of my life that remains a work in process. Yet I choose to believe that if there is a God, He understands.

Here's where the faith-rub is, though—the one I wrestle with continuously. If there is no God, then there is no Heaven. If there is no Heaven, then where did the spirit of Jordan go? Is it true, like my husband now believes, that once we die, that's it? Our loved one is gone forever. I yearn to see my son again someday. That is my thread of hope I need to covet. It doesn't make sense to me that, in some ways, I feel Jordan is around us all and protecting us. Yet if he "vanished," then how can this mystique of presence I sense be explained?

So, what I have *chosen to believe* is that there is a spiritual place where souls travel and potentially guard their still-living loved ones. I choose to believe that upon my death, I will be reunited with my son. I believe he will be reaching for me at my last breath. I choose to believe that there will be ways to protect my survivors and maybe send them hints of my love. I know it sounds crazy, but it's ultimately necessary for me to choose to believe these things. Why? Because it gives me hope. That's it. Hope that one day the pieces will all assemble and make sense. That one day I will understand why our family was chosen to endure this unimaginable ordeal. I need to cling to these ideals only to be able to put one foot in front of the other and carry on here on Earth.

Transitional and Ambiguous Loss

There's a phenomenon that occurs during a profound loss in which the griever loses not only the loved one but a peripheral circle of elements. I've mentioned earlier that the griever immediately is trying to rebalance their footing after loss—akin to a surfer on a wave. Their emotions are unsteady; perhaps their role has changed and there's a "new normal" ahead, which is much clouded.

What also occurs is that circle around them shifting with friendships, job interactions, financial impacts, and societal demands as a whole. Keep in mind, isolation, regret, and overwhelming feelings surround each element in its own way as well. No one is fully aware of these ambiguous losses except the griever—but often they are unable to articulate how they are feeling. The most simplistic way to describe these elements is collateral damage felt by the loss.

I share this passage because it's good to be aware of this type of loss creeping into the recovery process. Oftentimes, it will be insidious and not felt until the griever simply breaks down. Often, it's manifested by him/her saying, "I thought so and so would be there for me, but they weren't." When a listener hears this, it's important to let the griever know that this, too, is normal and will pass once processed in a healthy way.

Expectations of what was previously normal to them have shifted dramatically. It's just all new.

I felt this most when I returned to my workplace. I actually wanted to go back because the folks there are my second family. I needed them. However, when I returned, I immediately noticed them looking at me differently, with a tinge of perceived pity and avoidance. I was back at my desk, yet it was as if I had the plague. Looking back at this time, I understand now it was because my coworkers were afraid to approach me and say the wrong thing. But during that time, I felt abandoned and uncomfortable.

Thankfully, there was one person there who had the innate ability to give me what I craved, and that was my personal assistant, Steve. At his young age of twenty-nine, he was my life raft at work! I will forever be grateful for his ability to know exactly what I needed. You see, he, too, sustained a loss and was experienced for what lay ahead for me. Every morning he'd ask me a simple question: "Hey Cheri, how ARE you today?" He demanded a truthful reply. From there he'd know how to block and tackle for me the rest of the day.

But what was evident was that even with the passage of several months in that environment, it was not a healthy place for me to recover. I ended up leaving that awesome job for two reasons: I was not able to give the 120% I wanted to provide the organization, and they were unable to provide an environment for me to be what I needed to get better. To this day, however,

I have remained close friends with those who were my peers. At times, I feel a regret that I left. If I'd only asked for more time, or if I'd stuck it out, maybe I'd have an amazing career. But what I now realize is that if I hadn't left that position, I would not have been able to help others on this path. My world shifted into uncertain territory, but the quality of my life was enhanced! I live more purposefully and benevolently today. I think I'm also proud of the individual I have become on this journey. My life is 100% authentic. Perhaps, if I'd kept working on fast-track, it wouldn't have been that way today. I choose to believe that making that very difficult decision to step down was the path my life was destined to take.

The takeaway for this section is simply this: Be aware that there are other losses that are attached to the obvious losses. Recognize them. Give them a voice and process them toward a healthy outcome. Some may be around work, others around friendships, and even some around interests and priorities. It's all part of the loss package. Revere them as they truly are and deal with whatever you need practically; it is the best way to go through this element of grief.

Choosing to Believe

This is where I suspect I will lose many readers. But I ask you to just hear me out. During grief, there are moments when some folks believe that they have spoken with their lost love one, had sightings, or even had unusual circumstances occur that cannot be explained. I have to be up front with you all: I now am one of them.

The night after Jordan passed, we had traveled from Florida to New York, where Jordan lived. We slept in our family condo, although "sleep" did not reflect the restless tossing and angst. My husband was finally able to sleep, but I was so antsy. I decided to go into the other room and drift off at my own pace, watching mindless television. Apparently, that worked. But a mere two hours later, I saw a presence in my room that woke me up. It was Jordan stating that I needed to go downstairs, open my laptop, and begin transcribing what he needed to say. Amazingly, I did just that. He wrote (through me) a letter to our family explaining his last moments and wishes. Here's the weird part: I typed at proficient speed with no errors! The letter is three pages. I shared it with the family the next morning, and they were astonished at the accuracy of what we all surmised what most likely happened during his last moments. The pieces fit now. It gave us a degree of closure. Yet they were skeptical of the circumstances that led to this letter—as if I'd gone mad.

Since Jordan's passing, there have been many events within our family in which there should have been an untoward outcome. But we have continually dodged bullets. Most recently, I was in a severe car accident. The other driver flipped his vehicle. The reenactment of the accident shows that I swerved left into the car, whose driver was ignoring the stop sign. I should have been T-boned on the driver's side. Fatally. But by swerving into his direction, it spared me from death. The passenger side of my front end was annihilated. I walked away with a concussion and bruising only. *I choose to believe* that Jordan took that wheel and saved me. Just as I choose to believe he protects all of us. It might not be logical or even possible to some critics (which I totally get), but by me *choosing to believe,* it gives me comfort and hope that his wonderfully zany spirit remains with us.

Grief changes us. The pain sculpts us into someone who understands more deeply, understands more deeply, hurts more often, appreciates more quickly, cries more easily, hopes more desperately and loves more openly.
−Unknown

Pet Loss

While looking back over my life, I can't help but wonder if the pain felt with pet loss preconditions us for deeper pain ahead. I've been blessed all my life to have dogs by my side. In fact, I don't believe I've ever been without a dog in my family! It's true that dogs (and cats) have the uncanny ability to love us unconditionally. They are intensely loyal, compassionate, and comforting. It's unfortunate that they can only be in our lives for a decade or so. If given the choice, most people would want their special pets to live for a human lifetime. Yet death truly is a part of life, and when it's time to let them cross that Rainbow Bridge, it serves up a heaping helping of anguish. Any pet owner will tell you this!

When Gary and I lost our dear Gomez, a Chihuahua and pug mix, it tore our hearts to pieces. He was one of those special souls. We loved every minute of his thirteen years with us. His personality oozed out of every pore, providing over a million smiles and laughs. His love was palpable. He was ill during the last three years of his life, but we were there to nurse, inject insulin, and get up late at night to rub his aching back. We held him as he went to his eternal sleep. It was a passing that I would have wanted and that he truly deserved.

The loss of a pet ripples into the moments and rhythms of our day. You no longer have him at your feet; no more begging you to go for walks. Instead, you shake out his blanket, clear the shelf of his food, and donate the leashes. There's no more joyful barking as you walk in the door. If I were to boil it down, the *sound* of the home has dramatically altered. Gomez was not at all a noisy pet, but the *tip-tap* of his little claws on the tiles were always jovial and constant. Their absence is deafening. It is a fair statement to say that pet owners do indeed grieve, as do their pet brothers and sisters.

I include this chapter because anyone who encounters the loss directly or witnesses it needs to be empathetic to the feelings at play. Loss is loss. It's unfinished love. Gomez will always be remembered in our family. He's just not with us physically any longer. It does take time. It means to share memories as they arise. The grief process needs to flow. It would be a disservice not to allow whatever feelings arise to be seen, heard, and respected.

We lost Gomez shortly before we lost our son. Admittedly, there's no comparison to the grief, but there was an important connection to be made: the pain of the grief was familiar. The loss served as our lessons learned. We knew, from experience, that we can get through the curtains of sorrow. We knew we'd need to juxtapose our footing going forward. We knew there were practical steps to take to create closure and other steps to adapt to the new normal. In essence, the loss of our beloved Gomez provided my husband and me the perspective aimed at hope. We did know that we'd have better days ahead, but for right at that particular moment, we needed to feel the emotions that bathed our existence.

Just like grief, there are no rules for surviving holiday grief. Do what you need to do to survive. Honor your loved one how you need to and do what feels best for your fragile, aching heart. You are missing a huge piece of you so do whatever you need to do to find that sliver of peace.
–Angela Miller

The Firsts

I touched on the firsts earlier in this book, but it merits a revisit. This is immensely difficult for the griever to maneuver—especially that first full year. When we meet with "fresh" parents (those who have lost their child recently), what tends to bubble up is a comment about an impending holiday. They notoriously dread the date. Obviously, they don't want to be in a position to be appreciative of the holiday theme at that time. They just want it to pass quickly.

The special days that are most problematic are around Christmas, the lost one's birthday, the anniversary of the death, and wedding anniversaries. It goes without saying that any other special days can present discomfort. What we tell the listeners is to make a conscious effort to force themselves to do something special. It totally feels unnatural, but once done, it has wonderful outcomes.

Looking back to our experience, this is a non-negotiable for the grieving family to move forward. I remember when Jordan's thirtieth birthday came up in August. Thankfully I had eight months to prepare for the day. Our family discussed what we wanted to do, and we just did it! Jordan was an avid and skilled golfer. We live in a Florida golf community, and my sons and daughter-in-law were in New York. So, what we did was: I got some balloons, recorded a special song that resonated with our feelings, and wrote him a message. We then Face Timed the kids when we got to the 18th hole of the course, played the music, said special words, and released the balloons. It magically lifted our spirits!

I've heard folks do many creative, different commemorative things. The best way to decide what to do is have the family vote on a theme and research the Web for ideas. The more the tribute pinpoints the spirit of the loved one, the more it will come back to the family's healing.

On the Christmas after Jordan passed (or one-year anniversary), the family came down Florida to be together. We decided to get Chinese lanterns, each with personal messages, light them, and send them off to sea. Naturally, in Jordan-fashion, there was a breeze that took the lanterns back to us at the resort and blew all over—nowhere near the beach! We ended up chasing these ignited creatures so as not to catch anything on fire. We ended up laughing till we fell! It served as a reminder that Jordan's legacy will forever be part of our family's fabric.

There is one special person in our family's life who always sends us a text on Christmas Eve. This young man didn't know Jordan directly yet knows Justin, TJ, and me quite well. For the past six years, he quietly yet reliably sends all of us a sweet text, wishing us well on that painful anniversary. It's a simple thing, but it allows us to feel that our son and his loss is not forgotten by the community. It is a gift!

The message to be gleaned from all this is to be open to the celebratory possibilities for remembering your loved one—in an active way! Remember, they just have left the physical life but remain alive in our hearts and souls. They never leave us. Their love has imprinted onto who we are today. Celebrate that in any crazy, unadulterated way possible. Release those Chinese lanterns with zeal. The loved one deserves that.

Relationships are harder now because conversations become texting, arguments become phone calls ad feeling become status updates.
–Anonymous

Social Media

When the news got out that Jordan had passed, instantaneously our individual Facebook accounts blew up. We had been trying to keep ourselves paced and in as much control as we could muster prior to that. Then Facebook crept its invasive self into our lives. Don't get me wrong. I am a fan of Facebook, Instagram, et cetera. Yet during the raw times of loss, social media is that loose-cannon presence that envelops our family's privacy—no matter how hard you shield each other from its tentacles.

My son owns a tech company, so naturally Justin took the lead on most of the postings that came from our core group. For a brief time, it was respectful, paced, and soothing. Then the rumor mill, comments, and grief trolls came out. Typically, they'd post late at night. I'd awaken with my coffee in hand those early days to see the barrage of stinging threads. On the day of my son's funeral, I saw a thread that was nothing shy of cruel. Comments were laced with such uncalled-for judgment and venom. I'd had enough. I actually posted back to the group that I was his mother, that I'd seen the comments, and hoped that they never would have to endure the heartache I was experiencing. It took every ounce of energy I had to do this, but I knew that if roles had been reversed, Jordan would have done that for me, but in much more colorful language.

Then, most recently, I saw social media work positively! I was in Florida and saw that there was a tragic fatal accident of an eighteen-year-old in our small New York hometown. There were the typical comments, which seemed trite at best. I did not know this family but did know of the raw pain they were in. I commented on the thread that to truly help that family, contributors should send in memories, pictures, anything specific to that precious young man. Those posts would soothe the soul for the family members who would eventually read them. Immediately, the thread swerved to an awesome collection of memories for the family to eventually peruse.

My Facebook contribution went a step further. One of the contributors commented that I should consider reaching out to the family to offer real-time advice and comfort. I told the group I'd be more than willing to so but that I had no idea how to contact the family. One week later, the young man's dad reached out to me and a connection had been made between one stranger and another, all via social media.

Going forward, when we see a posting on social media, let's certainly unite but first step back, ask ourselves how the family would feel reading this, and then ask what the family would want to read. Let's use social media as a tool to comfort and create peace. Memories and pictures about the loved one are some of the best things a contributor could give. It allows the memory of the departed to live on!

On that same note, as a family we wrestled with whether to take down Jordan's Facebook page or leave it up. While this is purely a decision that is made individually, we left Jordan's page up. Years later, we see folks still contribute to his page with all sorts of memories, letters, pictures, et cetera. On his birthday and anniversary of his death, we get to read all sorts of things showing us that folks have not forgotten him. It brings us solace beyond words.

Grieving is a journey that teaches us how to love in a new way now that our loved one is no longer with us.
–Tom Attig

The New Normal: The Reinvention Stage

It's incredibly difficult to articulate the stamina and perseverance needed to traverse the grief journey in a functional, healthy way. In the simplest of terms, grief shifts our lives into a place where you are living when you are broken and whole at the same time. Our natural instinct is to curl up in a ball, pull up the covers, hide, feel self-pity, and believe that the world is a cruel place. At some level, for anyone who has lost, there's the self-talk around being the victim and thinking *"Why me?"*

The notion of fairness, equality, and joy with life has vanished. The onlooker will rarely see the griever admit to all this, as it equates to "not handling it well." The supporter will then try to correct their feelings. Remember what I said earlier: feelings are neither right nor wrong, they simply are.

I cannot stress enough the importance for the supporter to allow the griever to feel what exists in order to process. To correct them simply shuts them down and directing them more into that cocoon of despair. In fact, when I speak to others who've lost, I bring up this topic. It's important enough to give it a voice, acknowledge its possible presence, and listen. The griever will work through these negative feelings over time. We just need to encircle them by giving them the forum.

I'm not the poster child for appropriate grieving! I still am grieving six years later and second-guessing my emotions. Cerebrally, I know that whatever is in my mind needs to be there, as it is part of the journey. I need to work things through. Yet emotionally, I am not so sure. Early on, I went into that dark cocoon and licked my wounds that would never vanquish. I returned to work prematurely. I unreasonably expected more from those around me. I lost my faith (which I'm not proud of, but it just is). I expected too much from my husband at times. I became uncertain in every aspect of my life and its choices. I'm sure I was unkind to some around me. Most importantly, I lost who I was at my absolute core. That was the true collateral damage to this loss.

It wasn't until maybe year three when I was able to be self-aware to the person I had become. I'd say that I didn't like who I was at that time and knew Jordan would be incredibly disappointed. I needed to create my new normal in a fashion in which I'd be proud once again and look for ways to help others. You see, helping others is just who I am. I returned to the essence of how I am wired.

Remember when I shared that every day before our loss, I'd do a random act of kindness? Well, I forced myself to return to doing that, as awkward and disingenuous as it felt at that time. I needed to tend to me and what I needed within my absolute authentic core. Once I began to force myself to be who I felt I genuinely was, it became easier. It took every ounce of energy and deliberate living I could muster.

I share this because this is something a griever needs to try to do. It takes a lot to self-analyze and take inventory as to what feeds their truest soul. It was my drug of choice—to heal in a healthy, pay-it-forward basis. It may not be for everyone, but it's certainly worth exploring. Why? Because it goes back to a simple statement written earlier—there are millions of broken hearts around us suffering in silence. Why is that? It is up to us, those who experienced the pain, to reach out deliberately to these muted survivors. They need to be heard and seen.

I don't know when I equated the journey to a backpack of rocks, but that is exactly how it feels. I remember Jordan going to school with his prize possession of a beat-up, tattered, beige and red San Francisco 49ers backpack. He always had it stuffed with papers, snacks, and other things that were nonessential and old. He wore that backpack proudly as he walked every day to the bus stop. I'm sure it was heavy, but he loved it! Today, I feel that I am donning that same tattered and worn backpack, but it's loaded with rocks. To me, it's heavy, and some days the sheer weight holds me down. Yet I'm immensely proud of the journey I've taken because it made me a better person overall.

Since Jordan's passing, I have become a different individual. I left my high-paying career in medicine to nurture others in a different way. Being basically shy, I intentionally reach out to strangers when I see that they have lost as I have. I listen to their stories while I know it will simultaneously rupture my healing soul and packaged grief. I anticipate what they need and bring it to the forefront, and I offer them someone who understands.

A very dear friend worked behind the scenes and gave us the best gift of our lifetime—a bear wearing Jordan's tailored-down clothes. The bear sits in our room as a constant reminder of his lingering presence. Since receiving that gift, I have paid it forward, making around seventy-five bears, pillows, comforters, and wreaths for others, many of whom are strangers. I've created a Facebook page titled "Memories Held Forever" to share my creations in hopes that others around can see the simplistic designs and replicate them on their own for others they know who are going through this journey! Seven years ago, I never envisioned myself doing this.

I've taken old pictures of the lost person and compiled them into a published memory book, including fond recollections from folks in a workplace, stories shared, and feel-good memories. The book admittedly takes quite a bit of time to assemble and collect, but the final product is something that a family can cherish forever. Seven years ago, I never envisioned myself doing this.

Although I'm shy, I've become involved with community groups and organizations promoting healthy grieving. There are so many agencies out there that are trying to tend to broken souls, and they need volunteers and resources to sustain and grow. Seven years ago, I never envisioned myself doing this.

More important, as a person, I have dramatically changed. I'm very proud of how I maneuvered this difficult path and came through it with a new perspective. I don't stress over the petty issues of day-to-day living, and I appreciate those around me with fierce loyalty and affection. I sort out our relationships to only have around those who are healthy for us. I eliminate the "yeah, but-ers" from our lives—those who half listen to a suggestion while formulating their response before you finish, saying "yeah, but . . ." To me, that is a waste of my time and theirs. I move on. My purpose in life is now to help those silent sufferers as much as

I am able. Imagine if there were others in this world who could join my cause.

Grieving needs to be given a voice. It can't be shunned or hidden or ignored. It will happen to all of us at some point in time. Let's try to learn more about the journey firsthand and support those around us in a proactive manner. Let's not wait until they come to us—it won't happen. Bring up memories of their loved one every chance you are able! Remember, those who we have lost have not vanished from our lives—they live on in our hearts. Let's recognize that and celebrate the time we had with them.

Jordan's life at twenty-nine was dramatically cut short. But he's still living in my actions and intentions. He's here with me writing this book to you in hopes that some of the words will resonate and comfort or guide. I have felt his presence and message come through my drafts. He has prompted me to pepper some scenarios in this book that I would not have come up with individually.

I am immensely grateful for having him as my son. The lessons that this one child has bestowed upon me, his aging mom, are immeasurable. While the pain of his loss is with us daily, the gifts that he has taught me are incredible. Today I am a better human being than I was on December 24, 2014. Today, I know now that I have made a difference with my life by being able to support others in our same grief situation.

One collateral beauty gift is that I do not fear my mortality. I choose to believe that when my time comes to take my last breath, I will see Jordan reaching for me with his crystal blue eyes, pillow lips and silly sense of humor. Because I have been open to his messages and symbols of his vigilance taking care of my family, I know he's still in protective mode for all of us. I am pragmatic enough to realize that what I choose to believe may not be fully accurate, but it does comfort me. It gives me the strength to put one foot in front of the other without him next to me and yet still know I will be alright. It gives me the stamina to reach out to others who are hurting to tell them that they can go into that grief blanket and come out stronger.

I thank you, Jordan, for the wisdom, grace, and resilience you have instilled with every moment of my life going forward. Your life *and death* has been one of my greatest gifts of my lifetime.

About the Author

Cheri A. Copie, RN BSN CHC Is a licensed registered nurse specializing in healthcare compliance. But most importantly, she is a devoted wife, a mother to three sons and a grandmother. She wrote this book in honor of her late son, Jordan, because she saw others struggling with the isolating silence of grief. It needs to be given a voice.

Jordan was a decorated paramedic where his mission was constantly to serve those suffering. Following in his footsteps, she found herself proactively nurturing others with loss. She initiates those difficult conversations that many have found unable to articulate. Many had the same questions and simply needed to be heard.

Today, she's an advocate for the countless folks around us all who are grieving – providing the inspiration to share their loved one's life aloud and remembering them openly towards a more positive mindset for the survivors to embrace their new normal.

www.TheBookAfter.com

CPSIA information can be obtained
at www.ICGtesting.com
Printed in the USA
BVHW091356070521
606668BV00008B/1064

9 781662 909115